SHADES
of
GRACE

Shades of Grace

www.mainstreetoriginals.com

Kick back and enjoy...share... and pass it on... this is the collection you've asked for... I've tried to quote and give credit when known... if I've missed someone...I hereby "disclaim" with a good old fashion "I'm sorry"...I'm human...and will correct upon notification... and...although it will probably never happen...someone (and you know who you are)...once told me to take five dollars and buy myself a comma...lol...no

they say follow your heart...
but if it's in a million pieces
which do you follow...
strong souls aren't just born
they are built by going through
the most fucked up things in life...
and
still having the ability to shine...

Sometimes...
the only thing
standing between
you and
your thing
is reality...

everyone swears...
I day drink
and
say fuck a lot...

8

you know it's
going to be a
good day if you
haven't shaved
your legs
for nothing...

i am no longer
available for things
that make me feel
like shit...

Be who you were
before
stuff happened
that dimmed your
shine...

If you've
been drinking...
tell me
something you
wouldn't say
sober...

Yay...

now that is resolved...

my crazy can go

elsewhere today

"bitch mode"...
yes...
it's a thing...
and yes...
i can go there

then there's when
you go to say
something...
but ya...
you know you'd
better wait until
you're smarter...

this next version
of me...
doesn't
come
with
emotions

because …

I fucking

sparkle …

that's why.

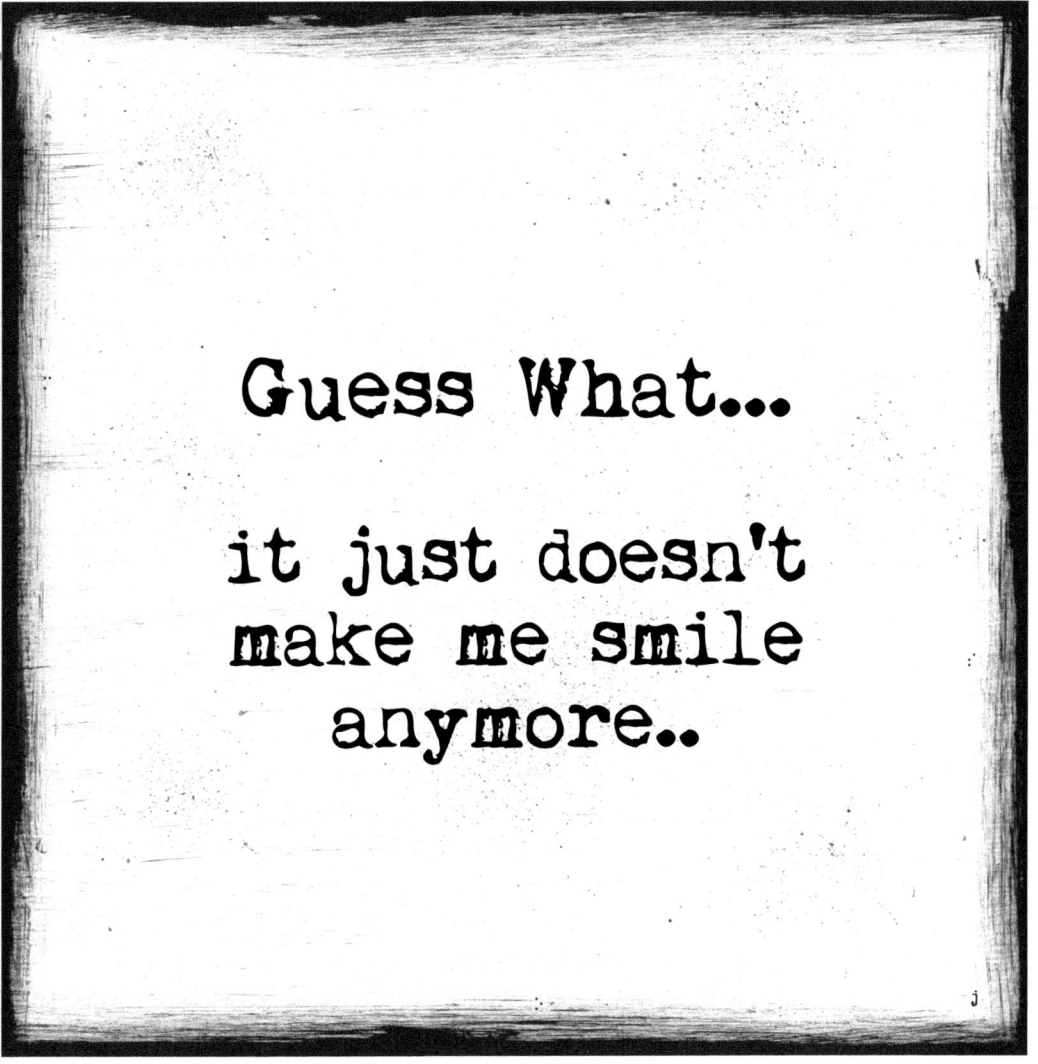

Guess What...

it just doesn't
make me smile
anymore..

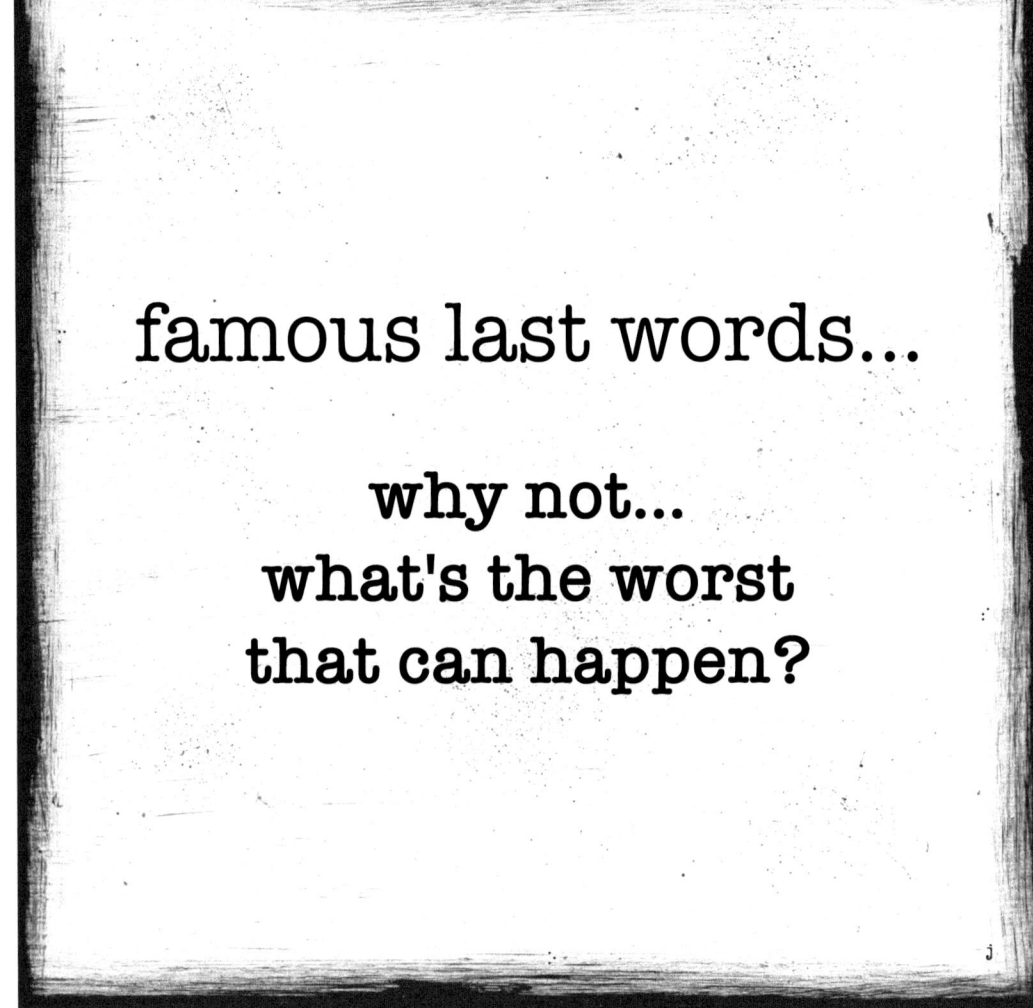

famous last words...

why not...
what's the worst
that can happen?

why yes...
I'm bilingual...

I speak fluent Bitch

Just sayin'...
no more wishing...
wanting
or
waiting...

I totally believe
in
"fuck off"
at first sight.

satan...
just
don't
fuck with me
today

j

Love is patient…
Love is kind…
Love is…
sometimes full of shit…

love days when your
only decision is...

will that be
in a bottle...
or
in a glass

do you ever look at
someone's text
and think...
ya...
fuck you

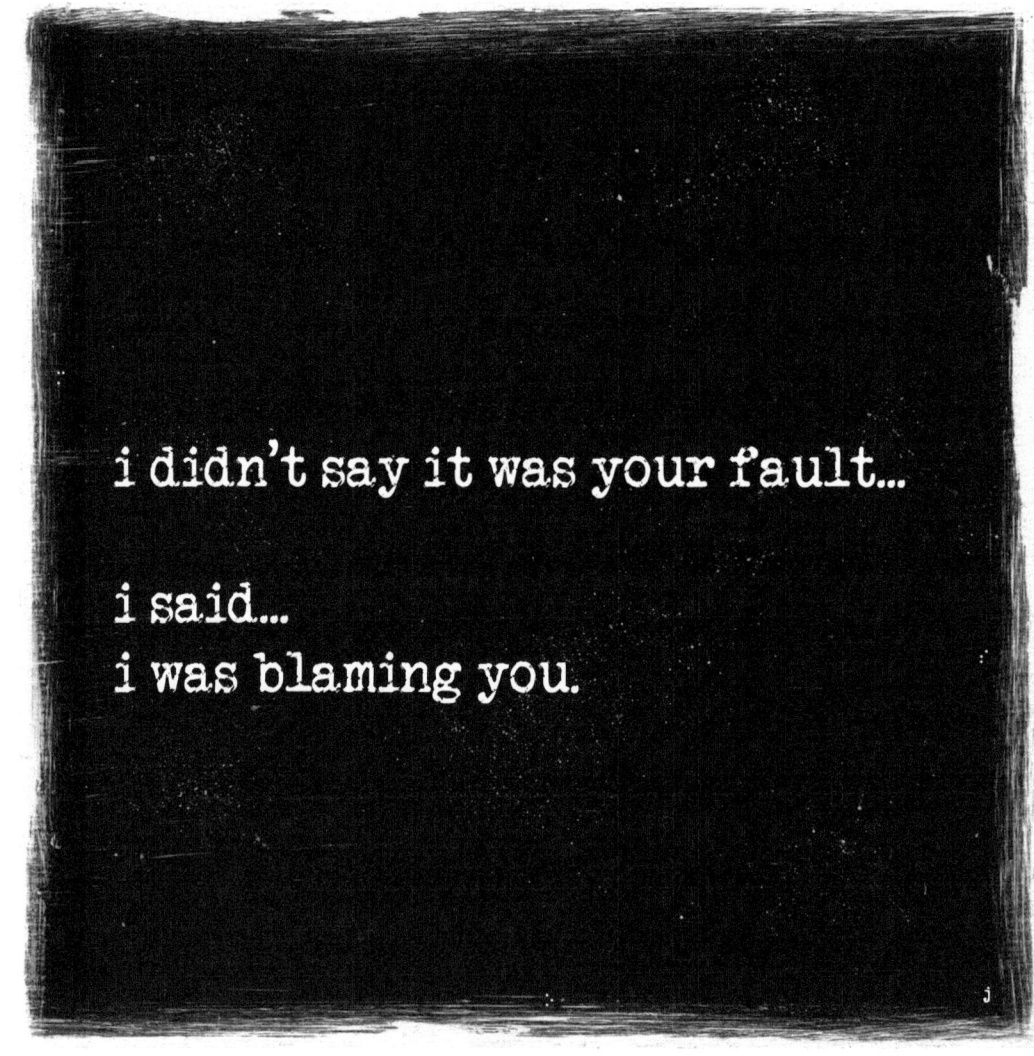

i didn't say it was your fault...

i said...
i was blaming you.

bless
your
delusional
heart

pretty sure...

i just don't give a damn anymore.

I see your silent
treatment...
and
raise you a
"fuck off"

being an adult is
mostly...
being exhausted...
wishing you'd hadn't
made any plans...
and figuring out how
in the hell you hurt
your back

Every
adventure...
shitty or not...
requires
a first step...

and... I get that
from the
drinkin' side
of the family

and...

wa la...

bite me

if there's the slightest
chance at getting
something that will make
you happy...
risk it...
life's too short
and
happiness
is so damn rare...

and...

we all end up
doing shit
we said we'd
never do

now honey...

she's not like us...

she doesn't say

"fuck"...

Cheers and big
hugs to those
who must deal
with idiots on a
daily basis

never let a horribly
confused man or woman
waste your time or energy

and... I really do
deserve more credit
for not acting
on the thoughts that
run through my head
on a daily basis

whoever is in charge of
making sure I don't do
stupid shit is fired...

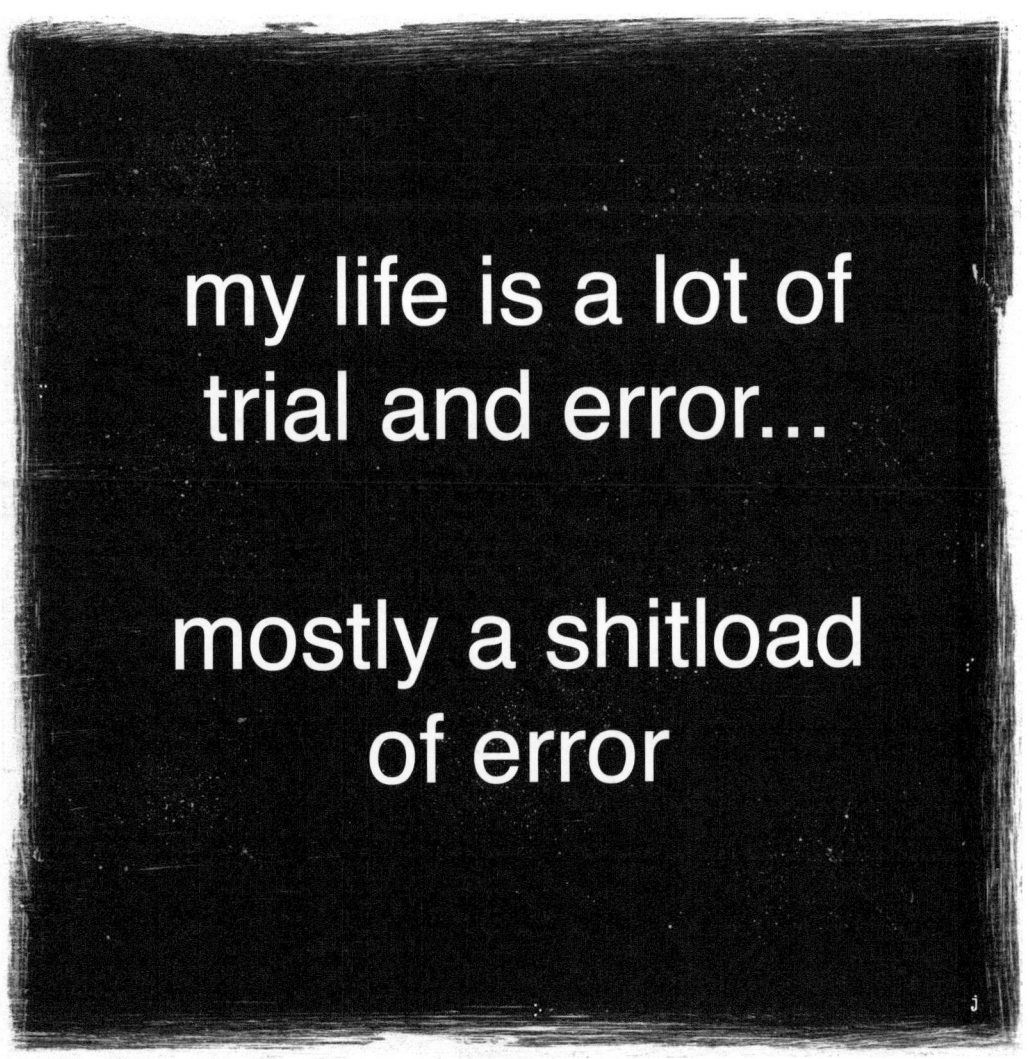

my life is a lot of
trial and error...

mostly a shitload
of error

and... i know...
my guardian angel
drinks...
and enjoys it

Ever wonder how
different your
life would be
if that one thing
never happened...
or if it did...

"fuck it..."

my final thought...
before making most
decisions...

best rel*tionship
*dvice ever...

m*ke sure YOU'RE
the
cr*zy one...

and...

they are all that
and
a bag of dicks.

I DO THIS
THING CALLED
WHATEVER
THE FUCK
I WANT

no need to throw me to
the wolves...
they come
when i call...

sorry...
this time
not sorry...

here...hold my
dignity...
i've got some
sketchy shit
to do..

stop complaining
about your life....
there's someone
out there
dating or married
to your ex

what's meant for
you...may only
pass you by
once...

karma...
is such
a patient
Bitch.

I've been told
I'm going to hell
for my excessive use of
the word "fuck"...
well...I've rented a party
bus in case any of you
fuckers need a ride...

J

everyone
thinks it...

i
just
say
it

not every

" i'm sorry "

deserves

" it's okay "

without coffee...

I wouldn't be
the perky...
delightful...
foul mouth...morning
person I am...

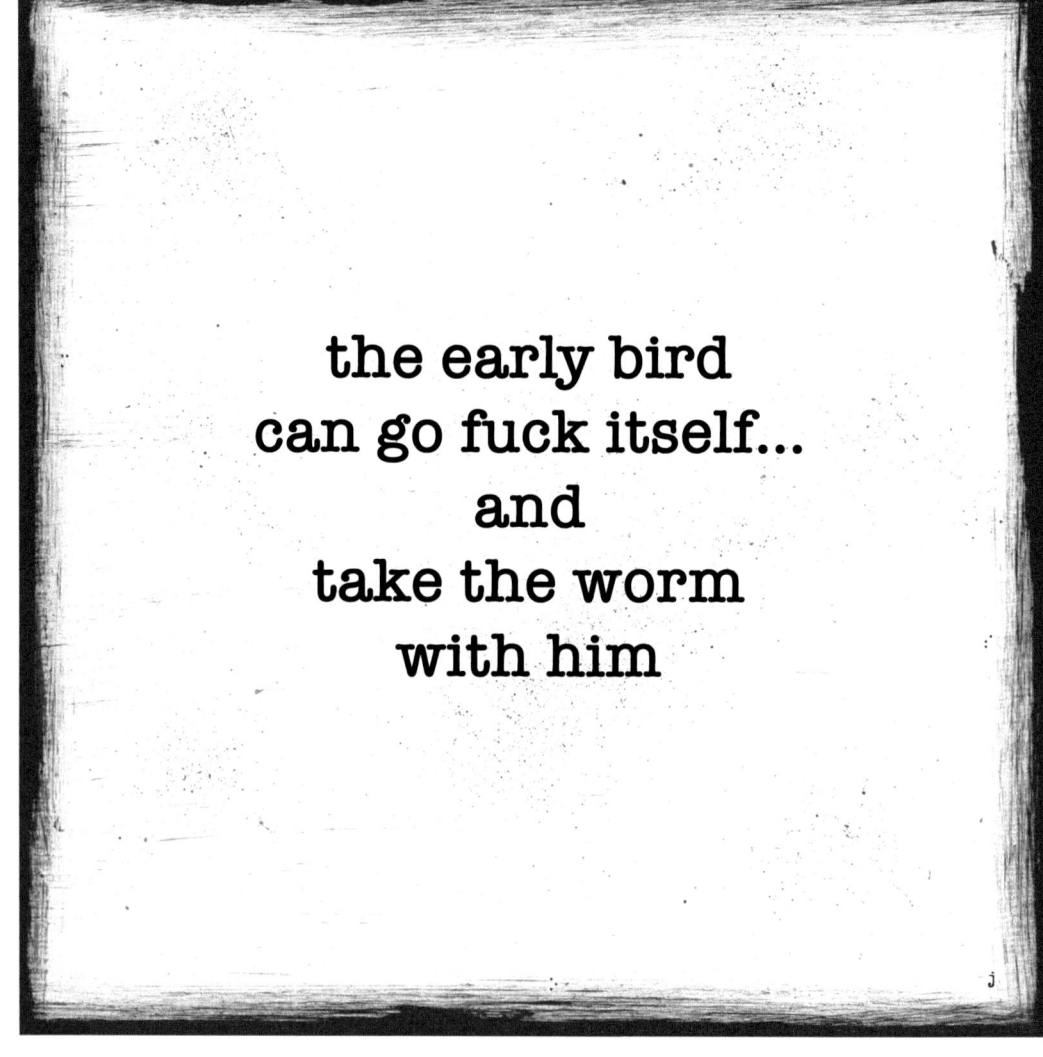

the early bird
can go fuck itself...
and
take the worm
with him

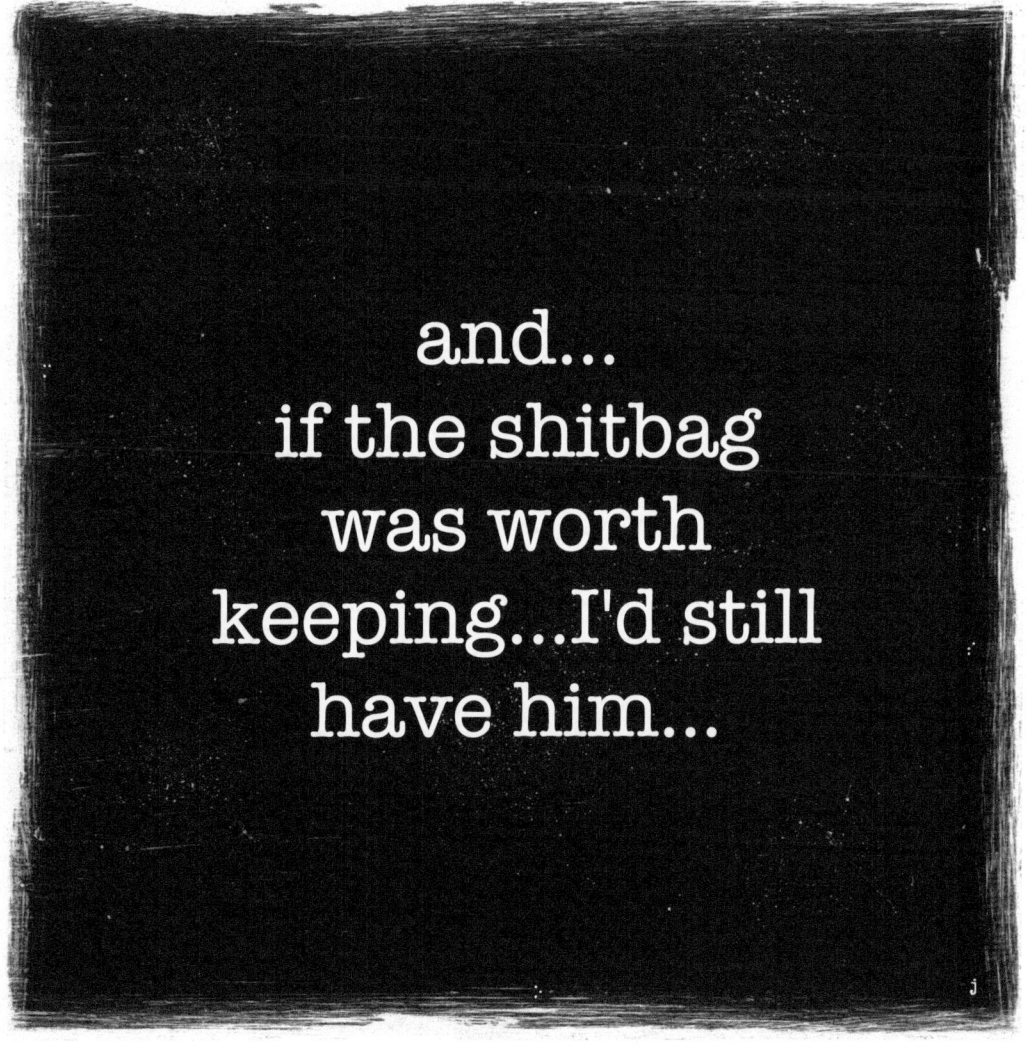

and...
if the shitbag
was worth
keeping...I'd still
have him...

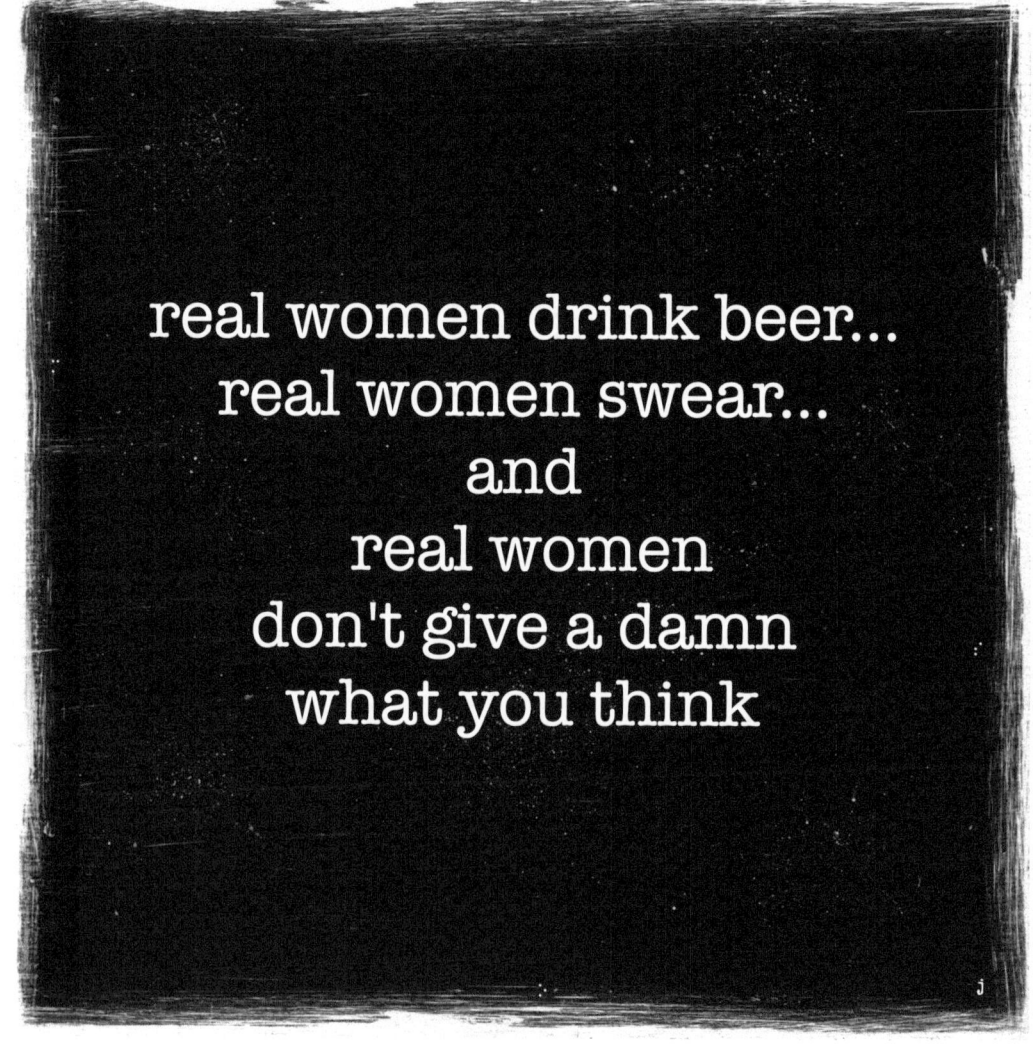

real women drink beer...
real women swear...
and
real women
don't give a damn
what you think

Behind every badass is one Hell of a story...

I HOPE TO ARRIVE
TO
MY DEATH...OLD...
IN LOVE...
AND
A LITTLE DRUNK...

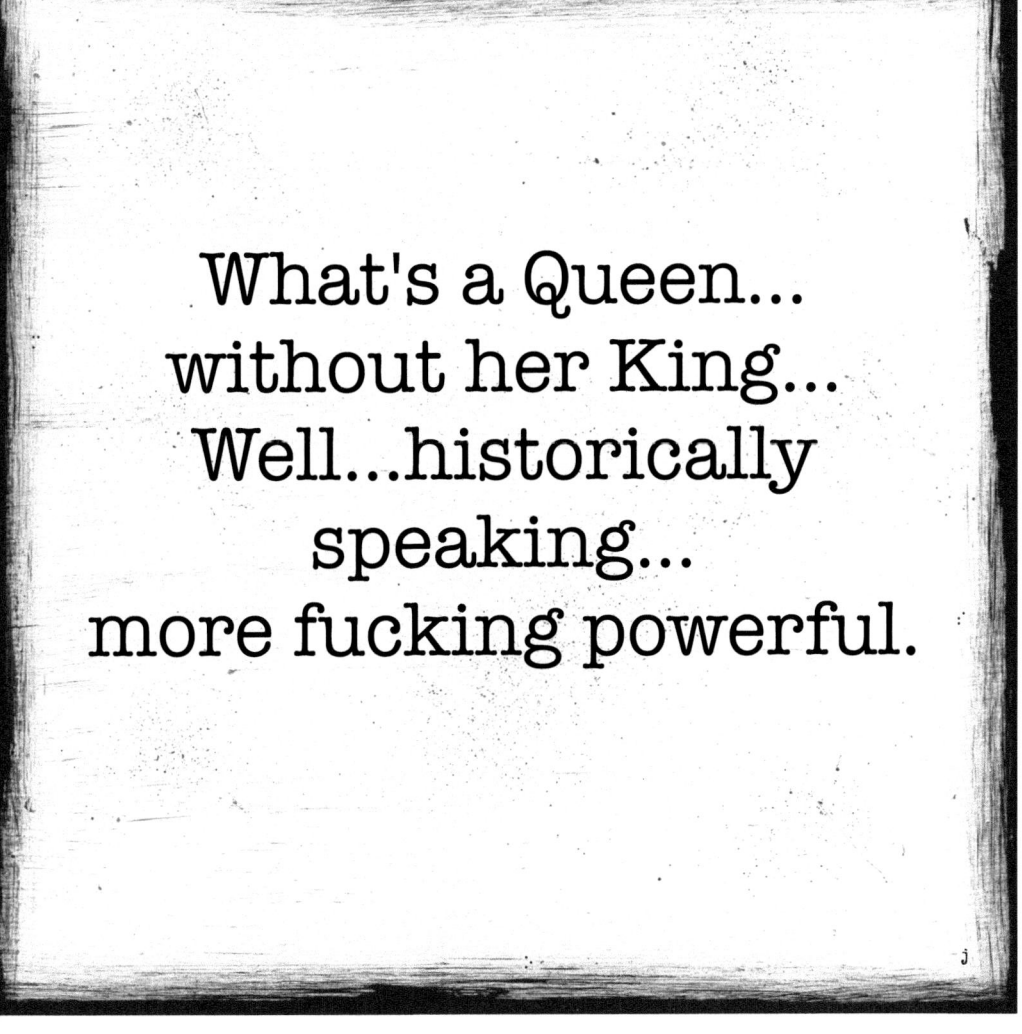

What's a Queen...
without her King...
Well...historically
speaking...
more fucking powerful.

i can look directly at someone...
nod when they are talking...
throw in a word or two...
and still not even hear
or give a damn
about a word
they've said

I am ninety-nine
percent angel...
but oh...
that
one percent...

66

Today... I learned that the
average person consumes
6 alcoholic drinks
a week...

Today... I also learned
that I am above average.

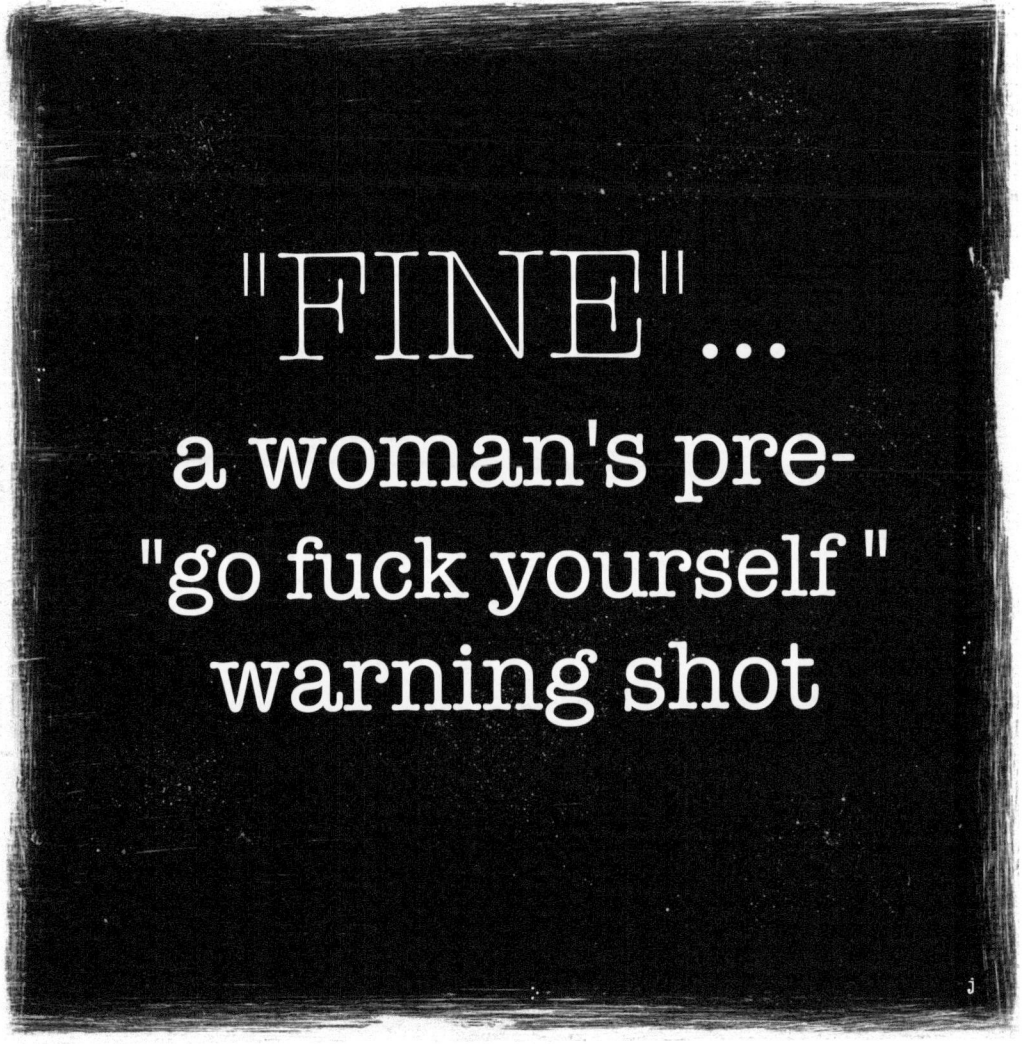

starting to think
karma has a
selective memory...
I see some real
assholes...doing
just fine

a fuck must be earned...

I can't just go down the street
with a bucket full of
fucks...giving them out to
everyone...

I feel that
once you've earned it...

I will give a fuck.

Time to manifest
the shit out of some
abundance...

I'M NO LONGER
FOLLOWING MY
HEART...
THAT BITCH
GIVES
BAD DIRECTIONS

I like the noise
you make when you
shut the fuck up.

I'M PLANNING
ON HAVING MY
FAVORITE
DRINK THIS
WEEKEND...
IT'S CALLED... A LOT

in reality...
all women are
crazy... so to the
men out there...
you'd better just
pick your
favorite type

I don't know where
all this crap about me
being a
"difficult person"
is coming from...

I'm a constant
fucking delight.

why yes...

I attended Catholic School...

Where do you think

I got my start...

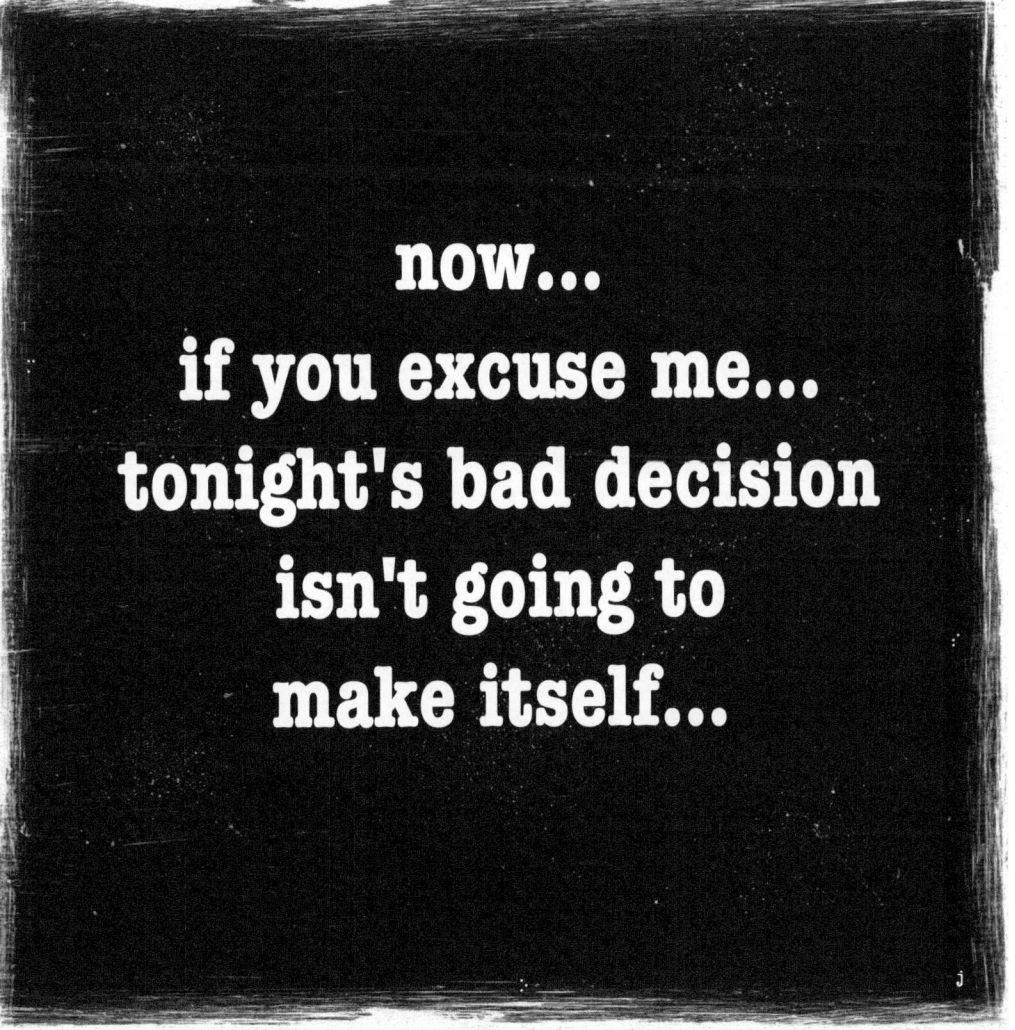

now...
if you excuse me...
tonight's bad decision
isn't going to
make itself...

learn some
manners...

apologize...
and
stop being
a dick.

fool me once...
fuck you.

I like to keep
things
simple

some mornings...
you just wake up
on the slutty
side of the bed

Your reflection in the mirror
should let you know...
You are a Badass

go ahead...
break my heart...
get yourself
haunted
for life...

set an example...
teach your kids
not to be assholes...

I whisper...
'what the fuck'
to myself...
about 50 times a day...

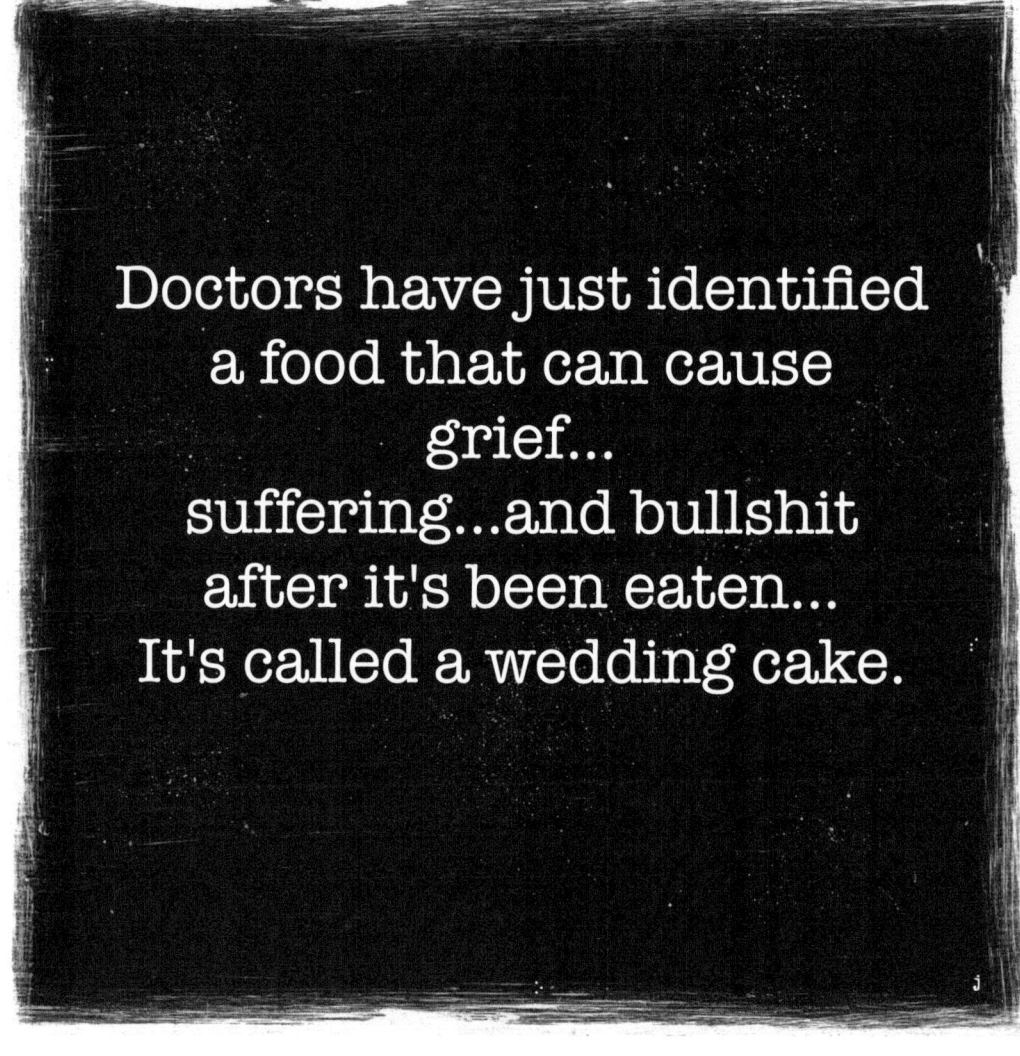

Doctors have just identified
a food that can cause
grief...
suffering...and bullshit
after it's been eaten...
It's called a wedding cake.

Do you ever
look at
someone
and think...

"Dickhead"

and...yesssss to
a side of
"musical chairs"

The Holy Trinity of Men...

He's taller than me...
Can F*** when I want ...
and
In the end...when I say it's over...
I get to keep all my own money...

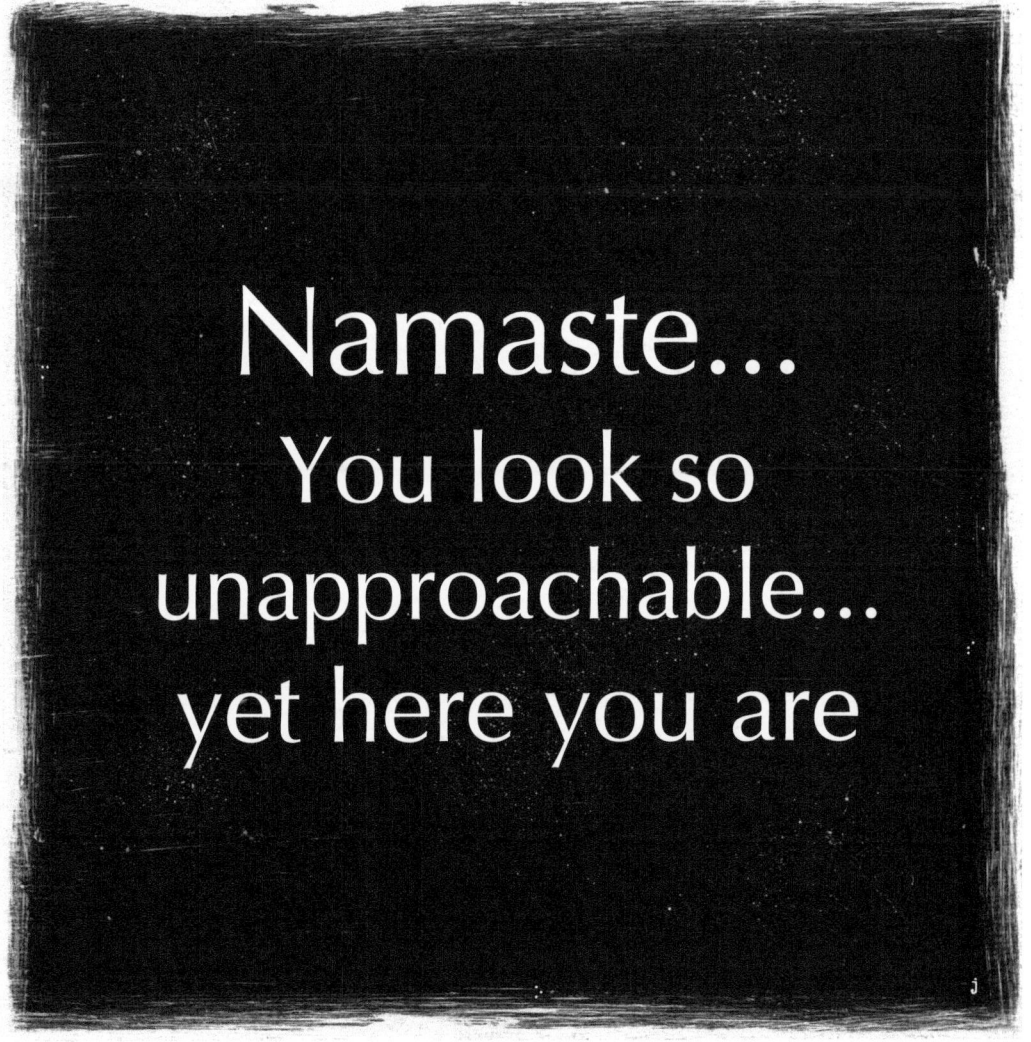

Namaste...
You look so
unapproachable...
yet here you are

choose

happy...

every fucking time...

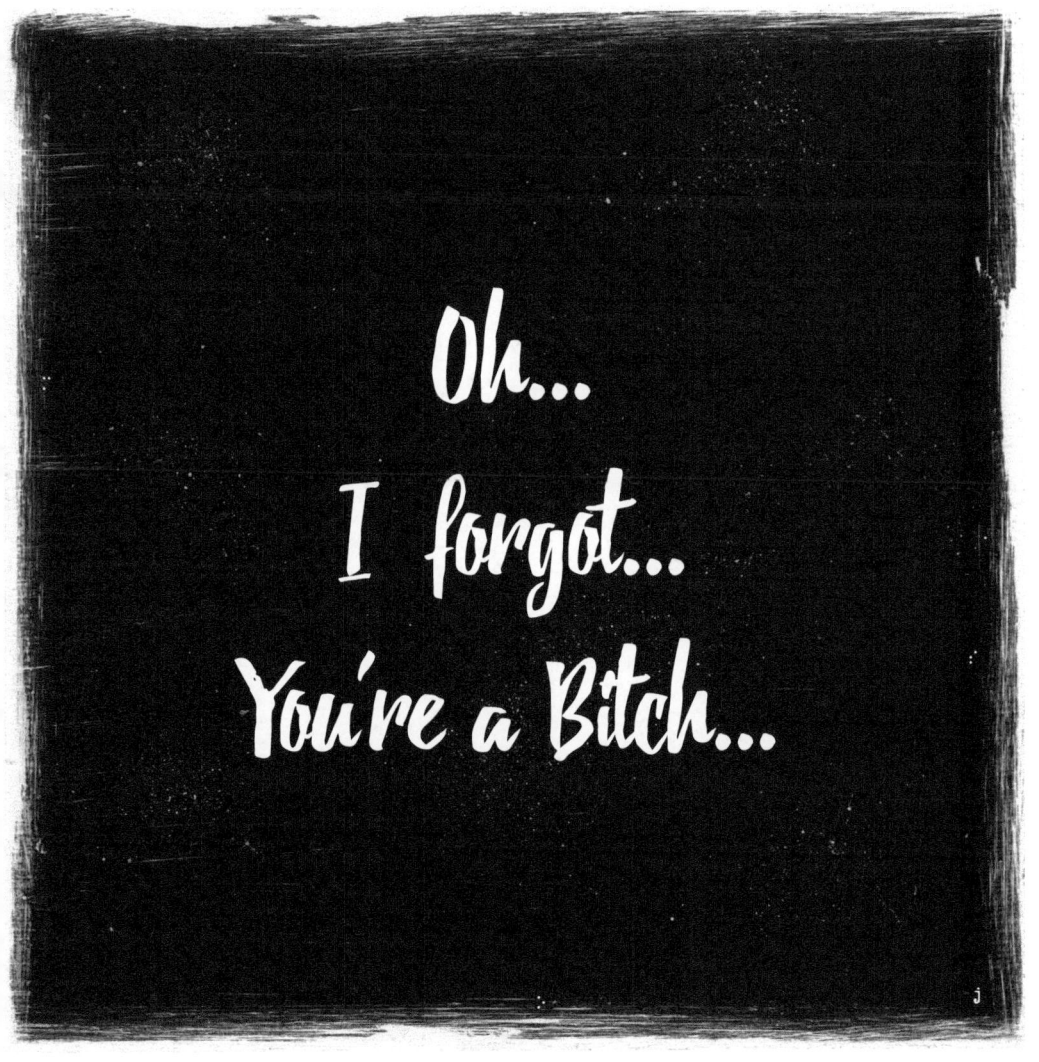

94

WARNING

does not play well
with stupid people...

You can always
replace the Head
of your
War Department...

because you're married to her

Smile...

wave...

and

say...

Bitchhh.

Cut Off...
all the
Iffy Ones

I want to be 20 again
and ruin my life
differently...
I have a few
new ideas

We are just...
intelligent...
classy...well educated
women who happen to
screw... a lot

even if I
lowered my
expectations...
you still
wouldn't
make the cut...

J

and maybe...
you should
just go fuck
yourself...

bitch...

I will mess your
day up
with a smile on my
face...

103

and...

guess what...

she does own

the place

"bitchy dust"...
is
such
a
real
thing

hey...
You look like a
really
Bad Decision...
Get the fuck
over here...

And...in the end...

Karma

will be a bigger Bitch

than Me...!

big girls don't cry...

we pop a couple of Xanax...
wash em' down with
some beer...bourbon...vodka
and wine...
then set your truck on fire...
don't even ask what happens
when tequilla is added...

fun fact:
alcohol nearly
triples the size
of the "Send"
button...

He could even
fuck up
a wet dream...

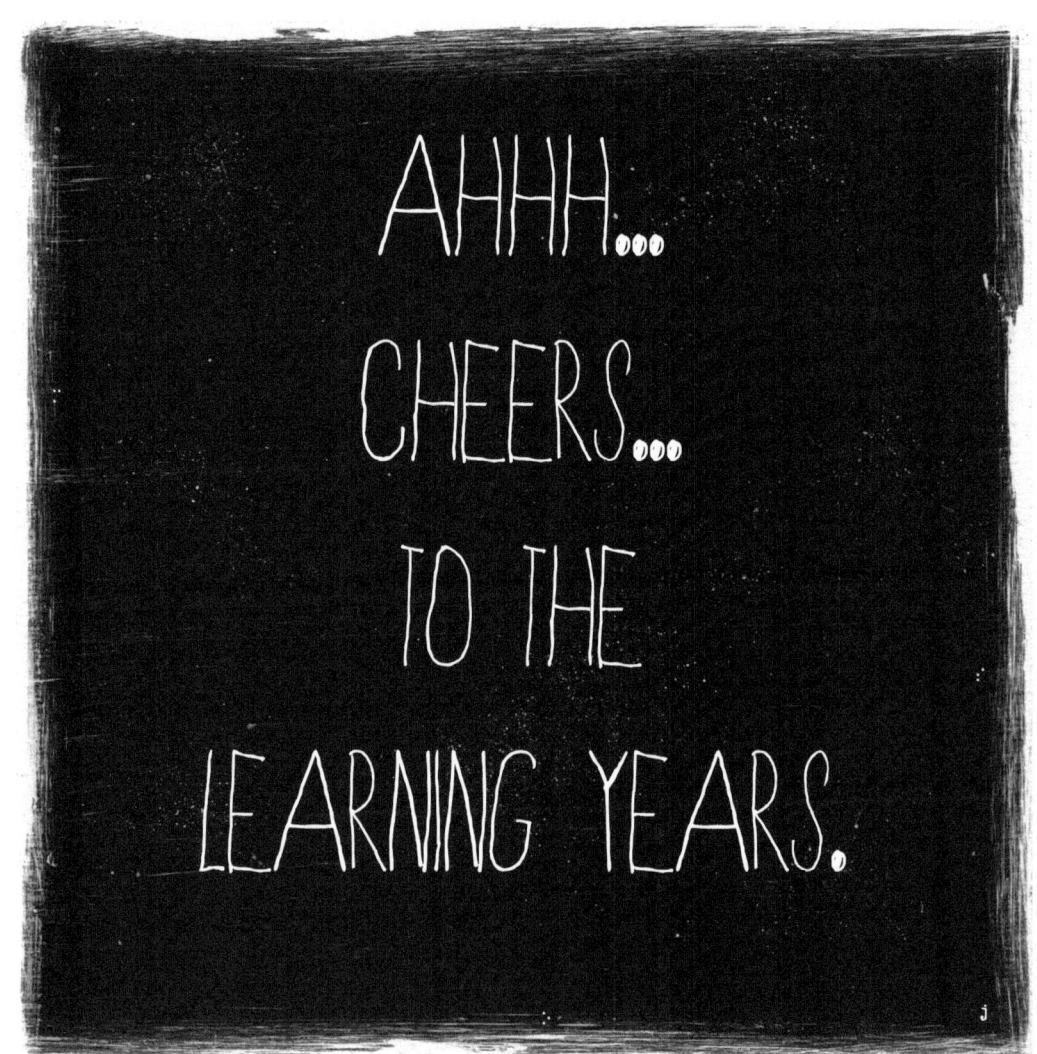

Fuck...

still my favorite unit of ...

time... measurement... and

attitude.

treat me like
an option...
You...
my friend...
leave me the
perfect choice

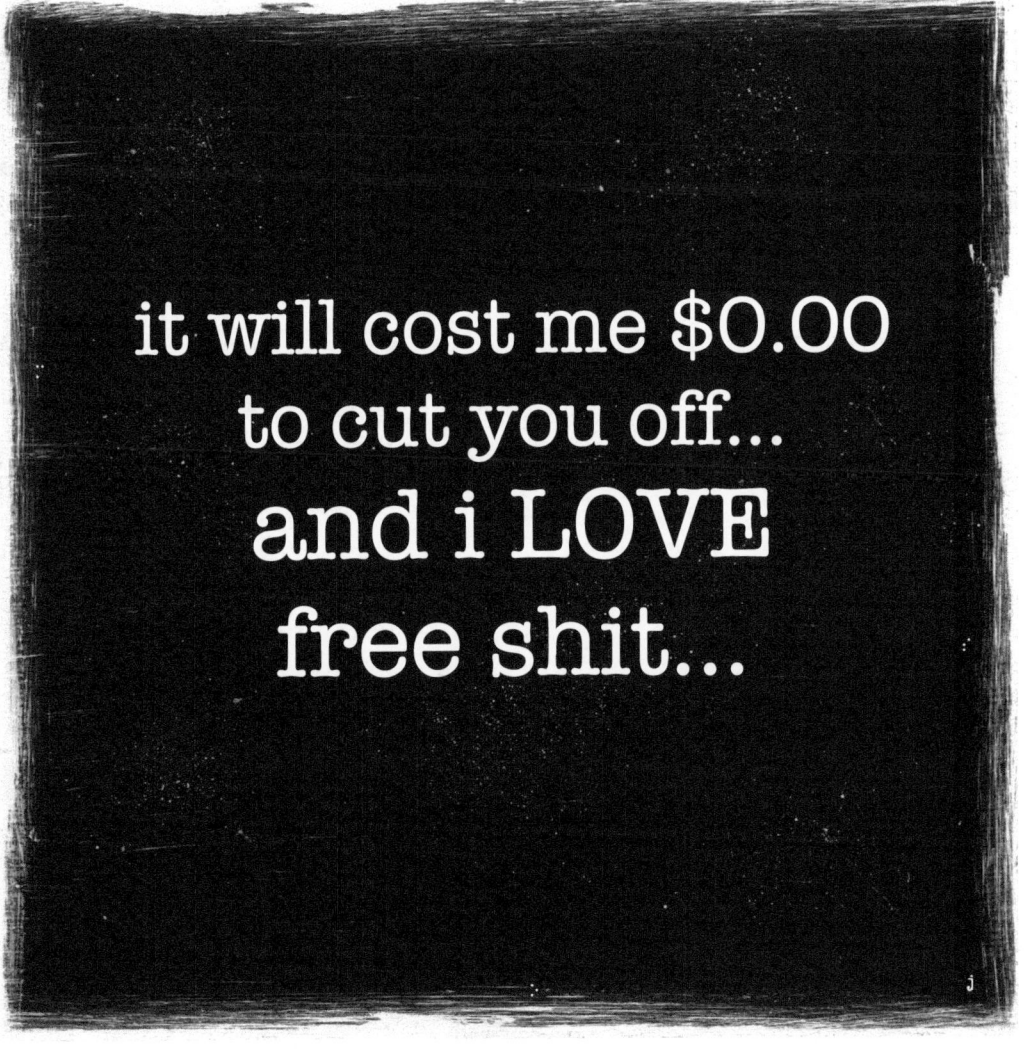

it will cost me $0.00
to cut you off...
and i LOVE
free shit...

her...
oooh do that thing I love...
him...
ok... what do you want
on your pizza

My boss is
sooooo
mad at me...
I keep calling
him Dick...
his name is
Bob...

I'm pretty sure
I had a good time
last night...
I'm waiting for
someone to tell me
about it...
or read the police
report

I finally quit
drinking for
good...
now it is just
for evil...

I'm a nice person...
So if I'm a Bitch
to you... you'll
need to ask yourself why

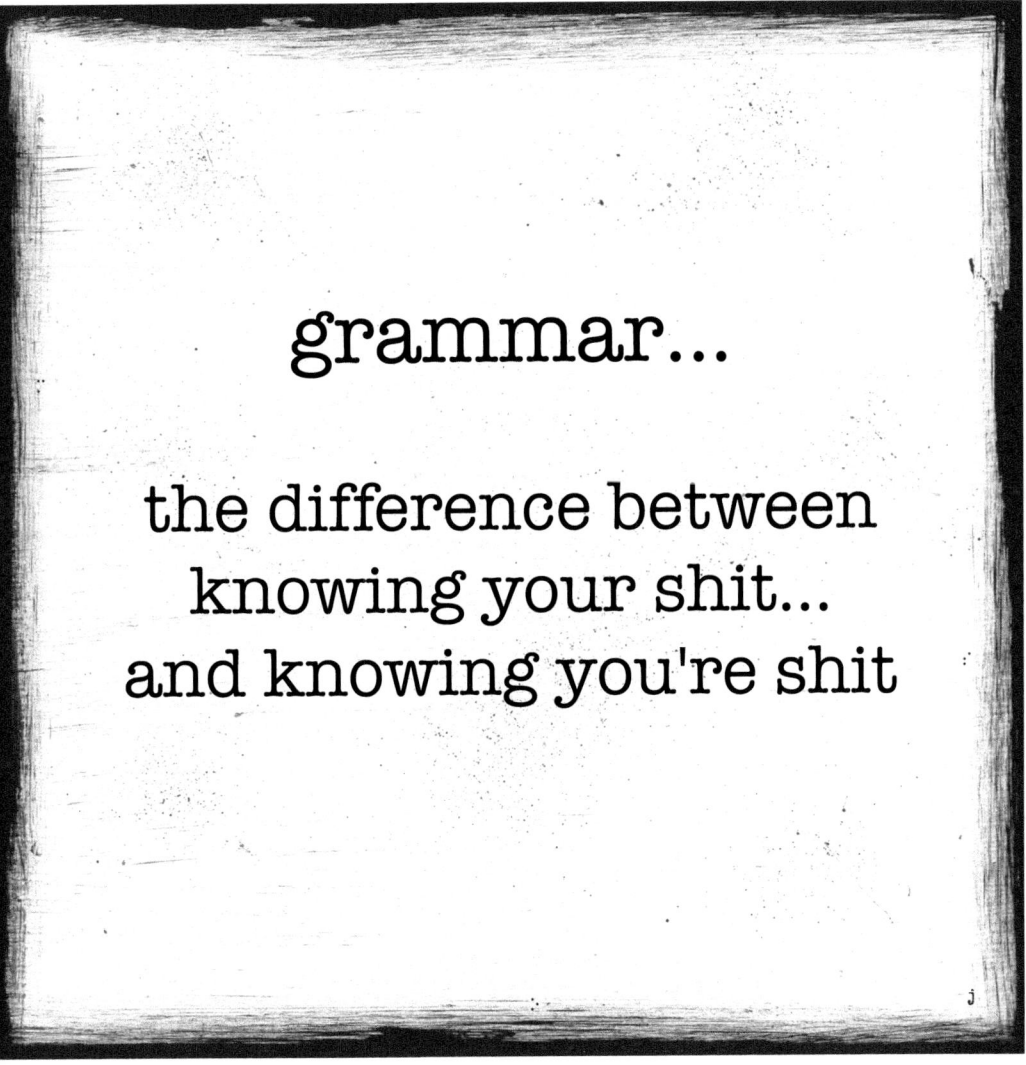

grammar...

the difference between
knowing your shit...
and knowing you're shit

Note to Self...
let the
bullshit go.

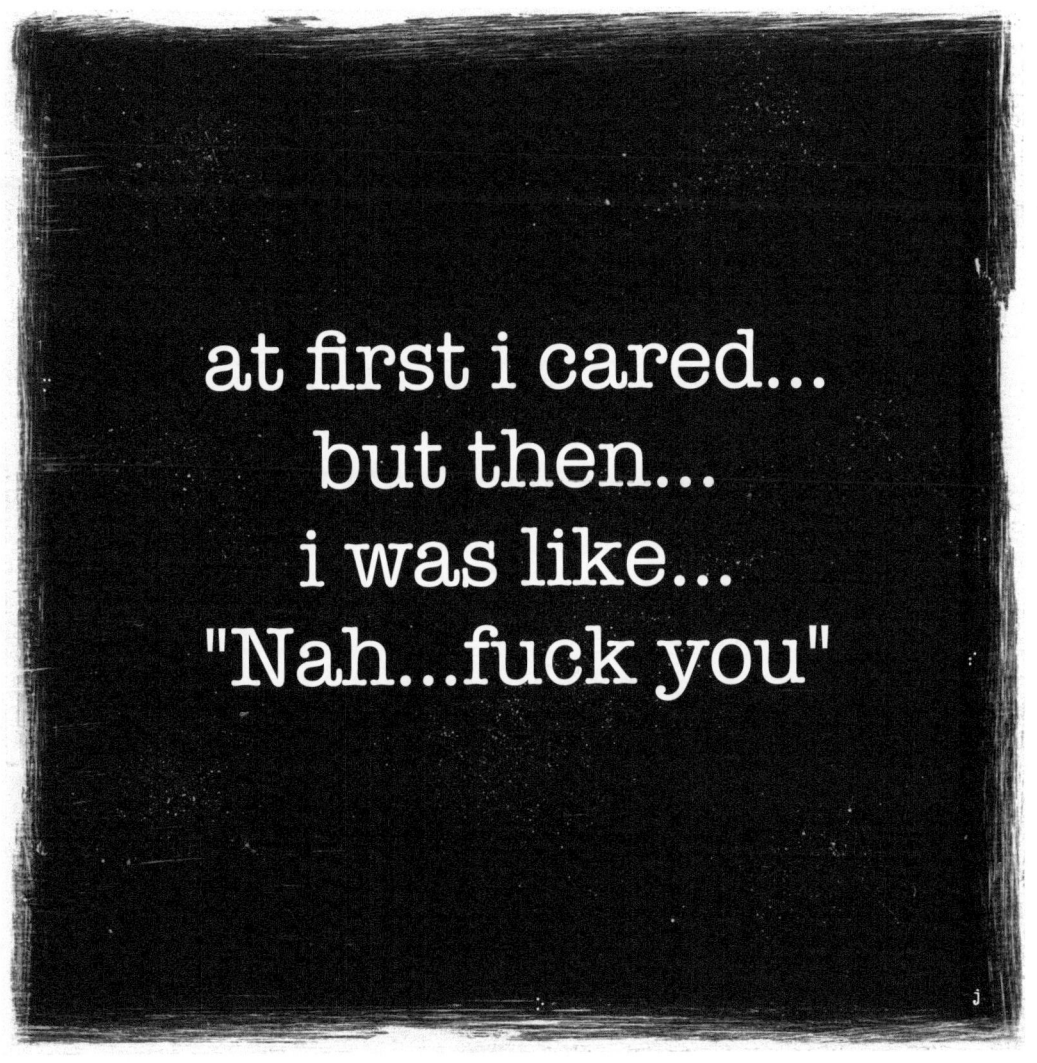

at first i cared...
but then...
i was like...
"Nah...fuck you"

I hate days
that blow up in
your face then
turn around and
bite you
in the ass...

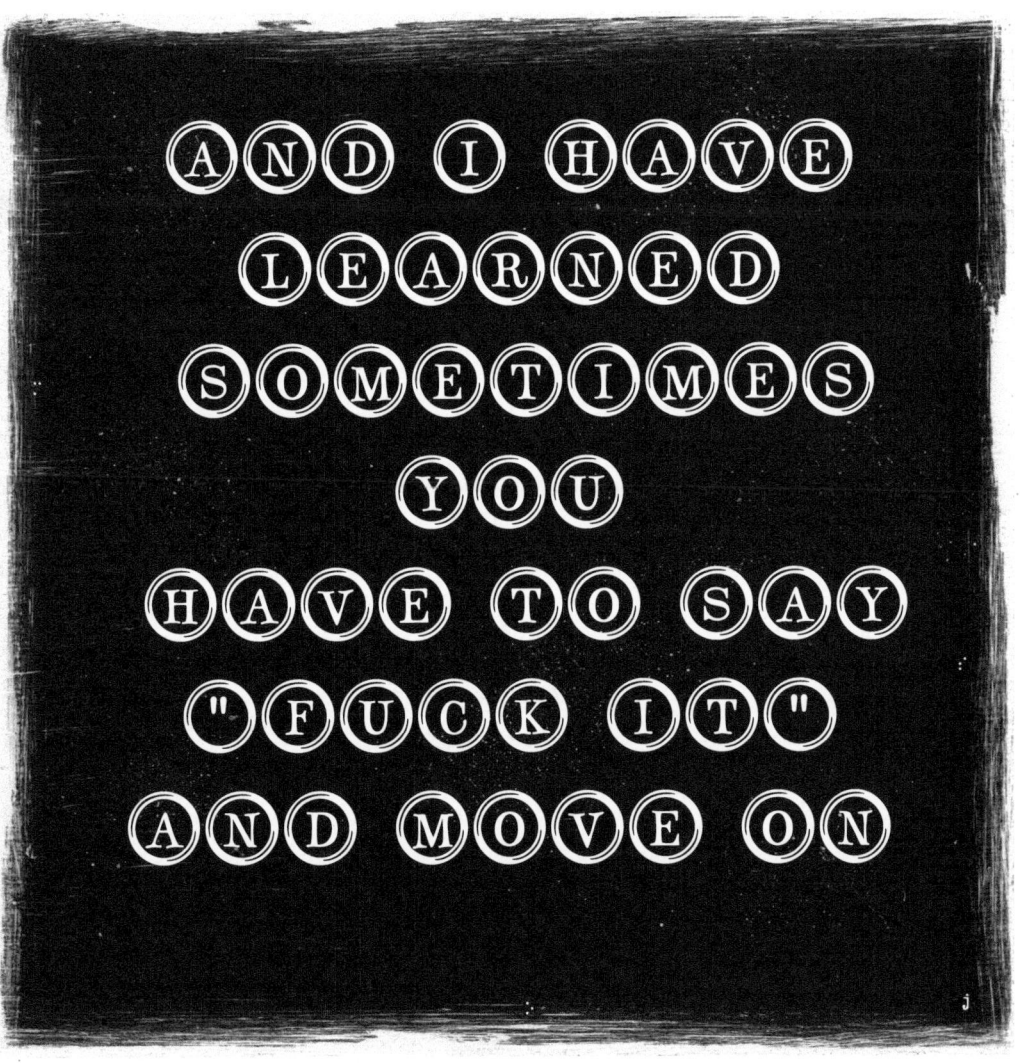

AND I HAVE LEARNED SOMETIMES YOU HAVE TO SAY "FUCK IT" AND MOVE ON

have you ever walked
past a mirror and had that
'rode hard...put away wet'
look
and haven't been...

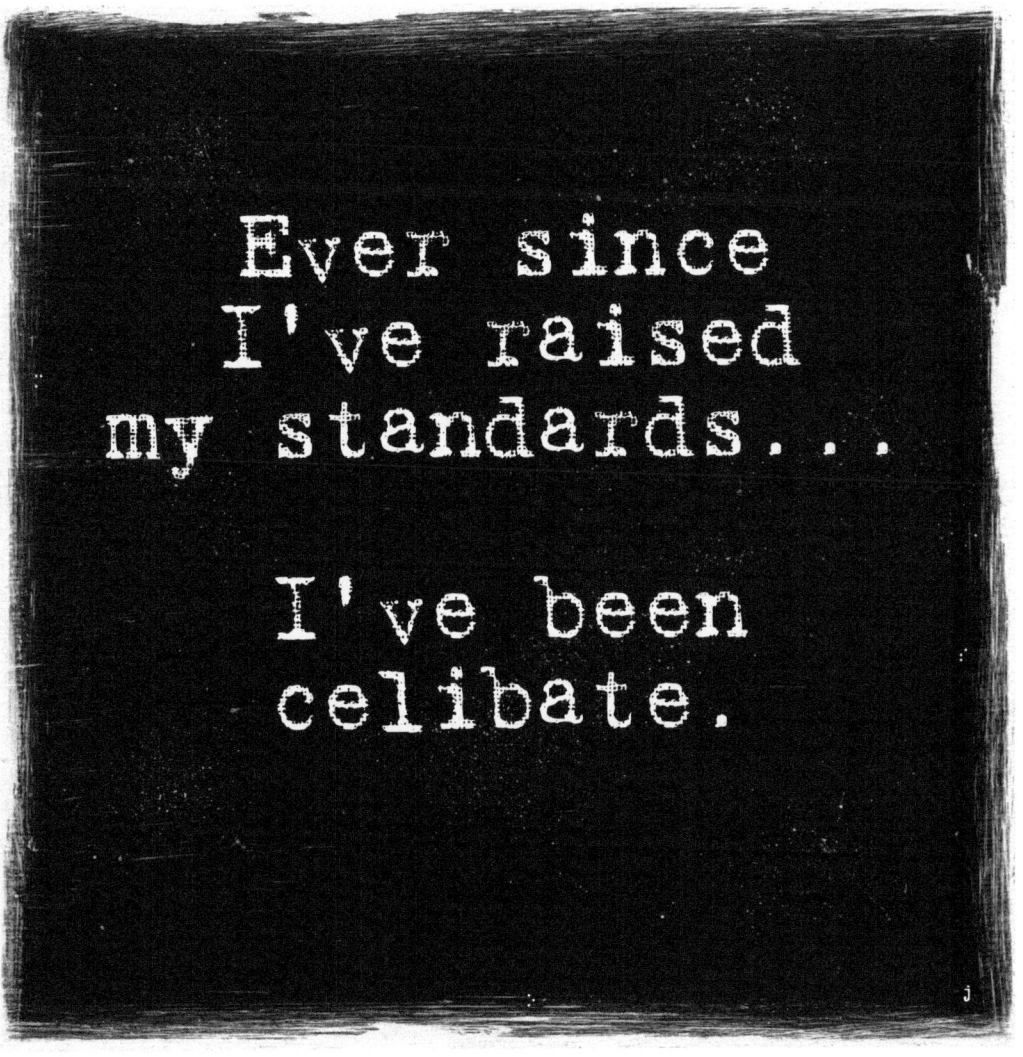

Ever since
I've raised
my standards...

I've been
celibate.

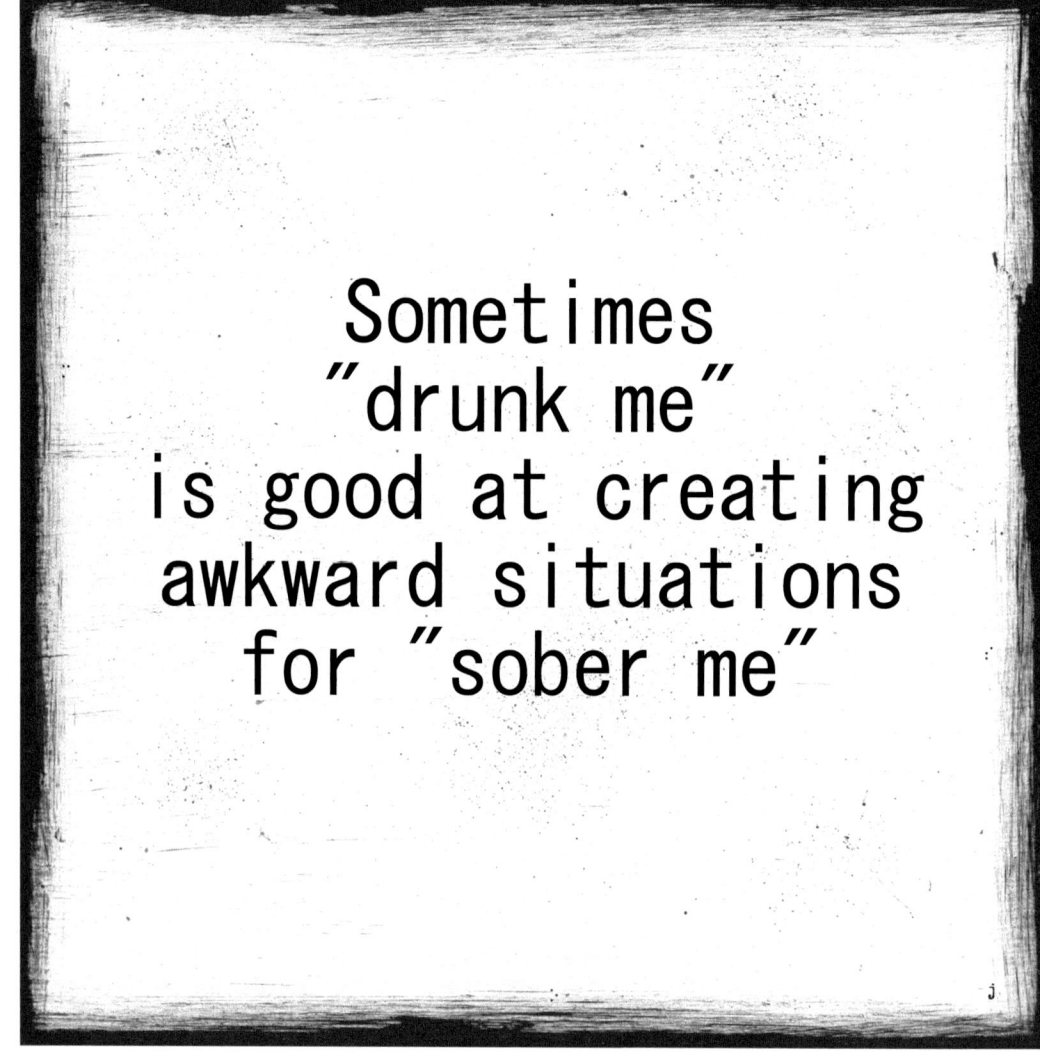

Sometimes
"drunk me"
is good at creating
awkward situations
for "sober me"

128

It's called Karma
and it's
pronounced...

"Ha Ha... fuck you"

i'm not sure how many times a therapist is supposed to say "Wow" in the first session...but yep... here we are... "Wow"

Hey girl...

that high horse

makes your ass

look big.

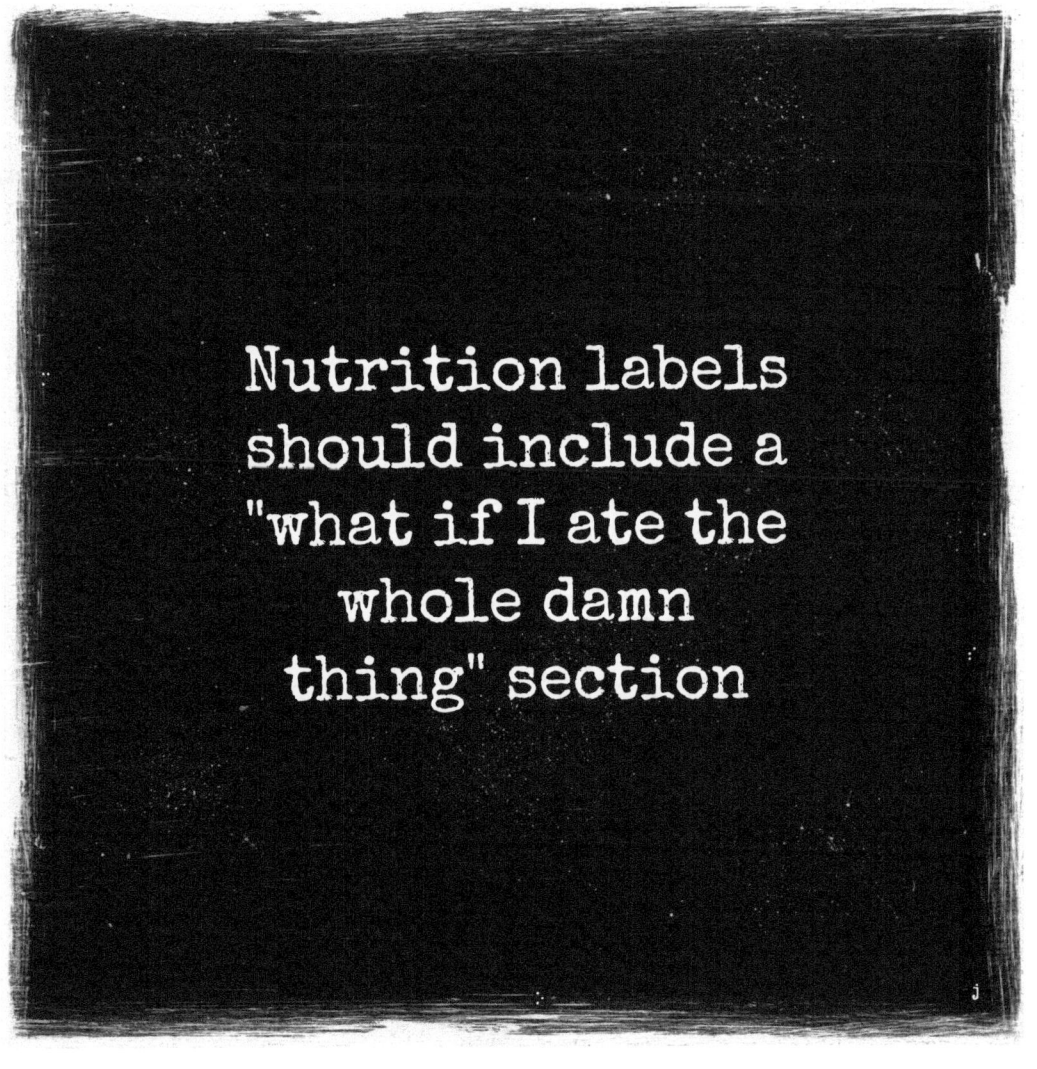

Nutrition labels
should include a
"what if I ate the
whole damn
thing" section

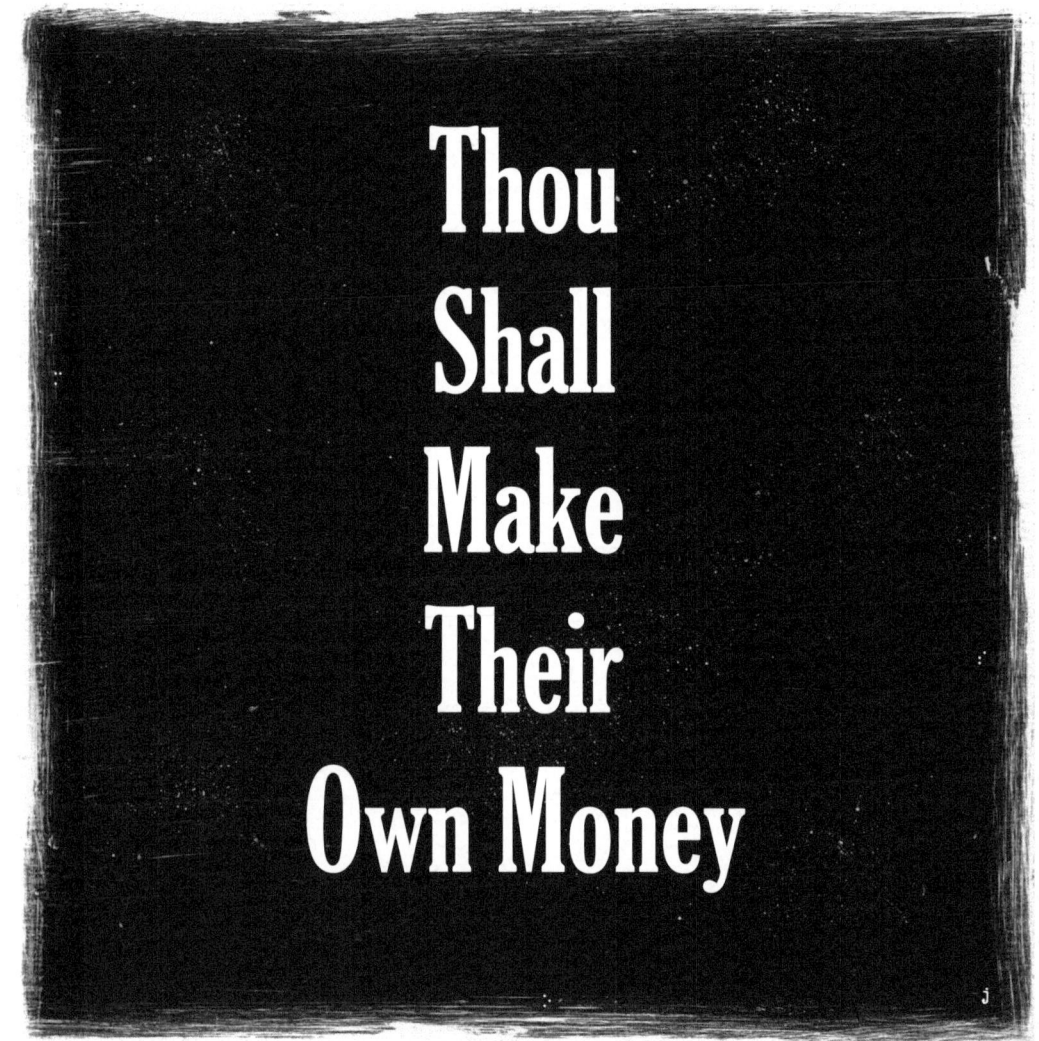

Thou
Shall
Make
Their
Own Money

and... hey... back off...

i've got enough going on

today without having to

worry about how to make

your death look like an

accident...

Asking for a friend...
what does it mean if
holy water
sizzles when it hits
your skin

ready for my
next toxic
relationship...
where you at
psycho?

Hey ...
My dog and I
talk shit about
you...

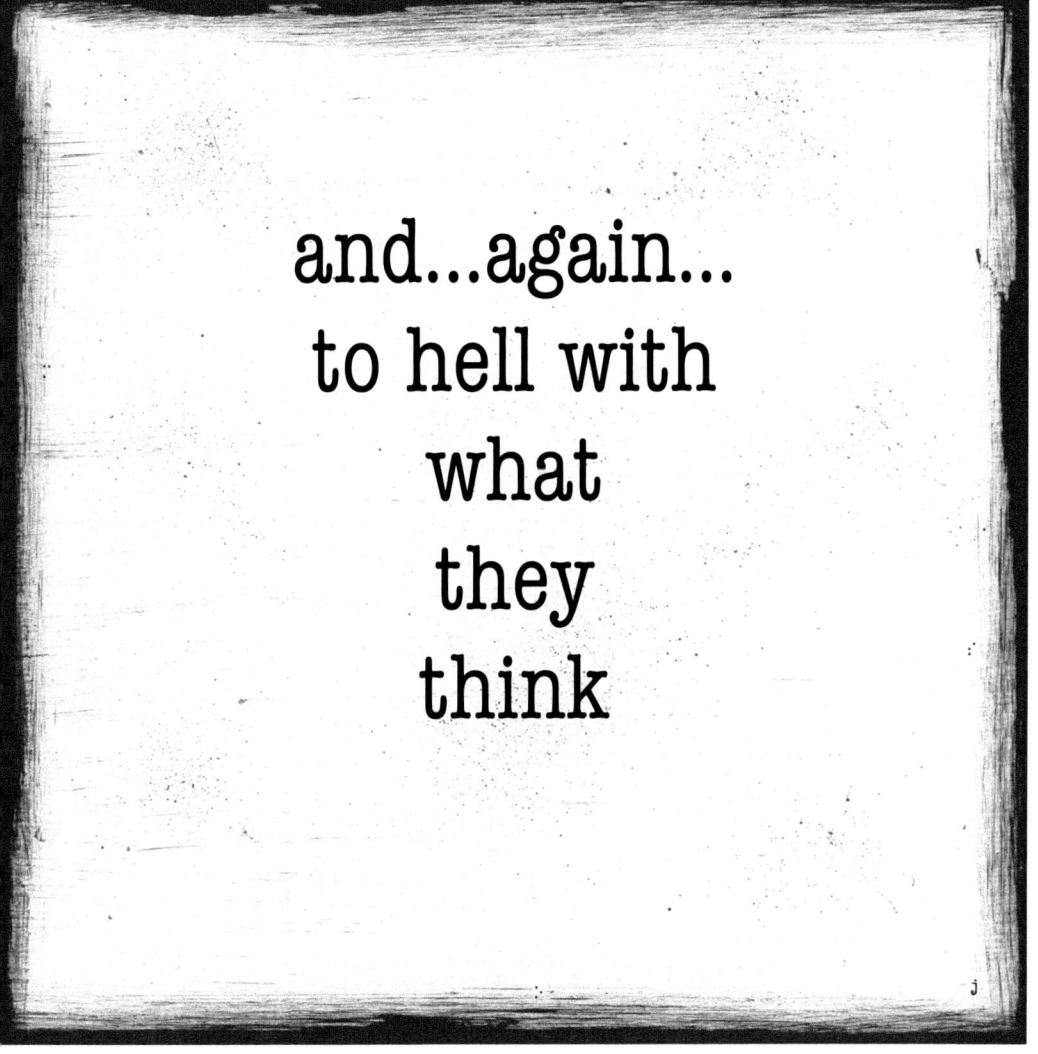

and...again...
to hell with
what
they
think

never settle for...
shitty coffee...
shitty men...
or
shitty friends.

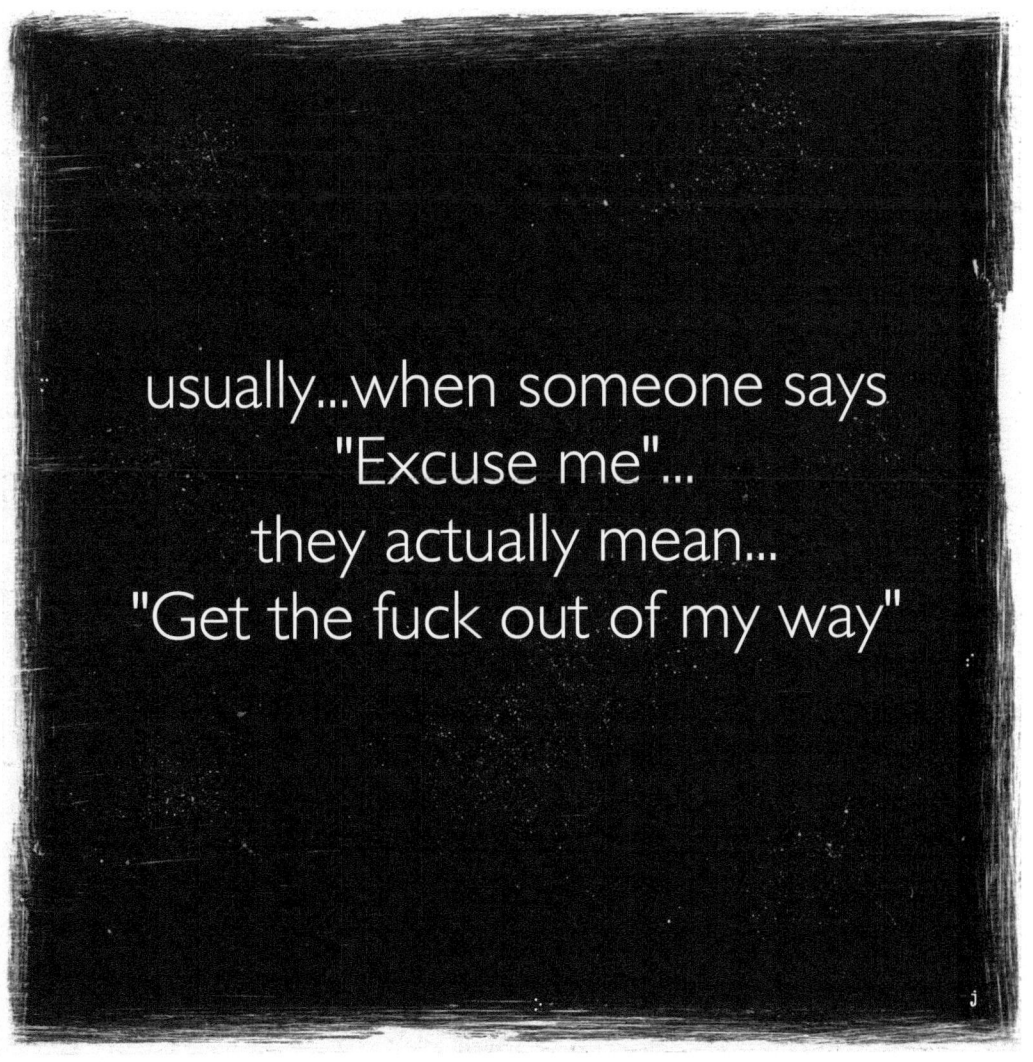

usually...when someone says
"Excuse me"...
they actually mean...
"Get the fuck out of my way"

140

i am in charge
of how i feel...
and today i am
choosing totally
BITCHY.

married men...
somebody
else's
problem

Nothing is more dangerous than a woman with a beautiful mind that isn't afraid.

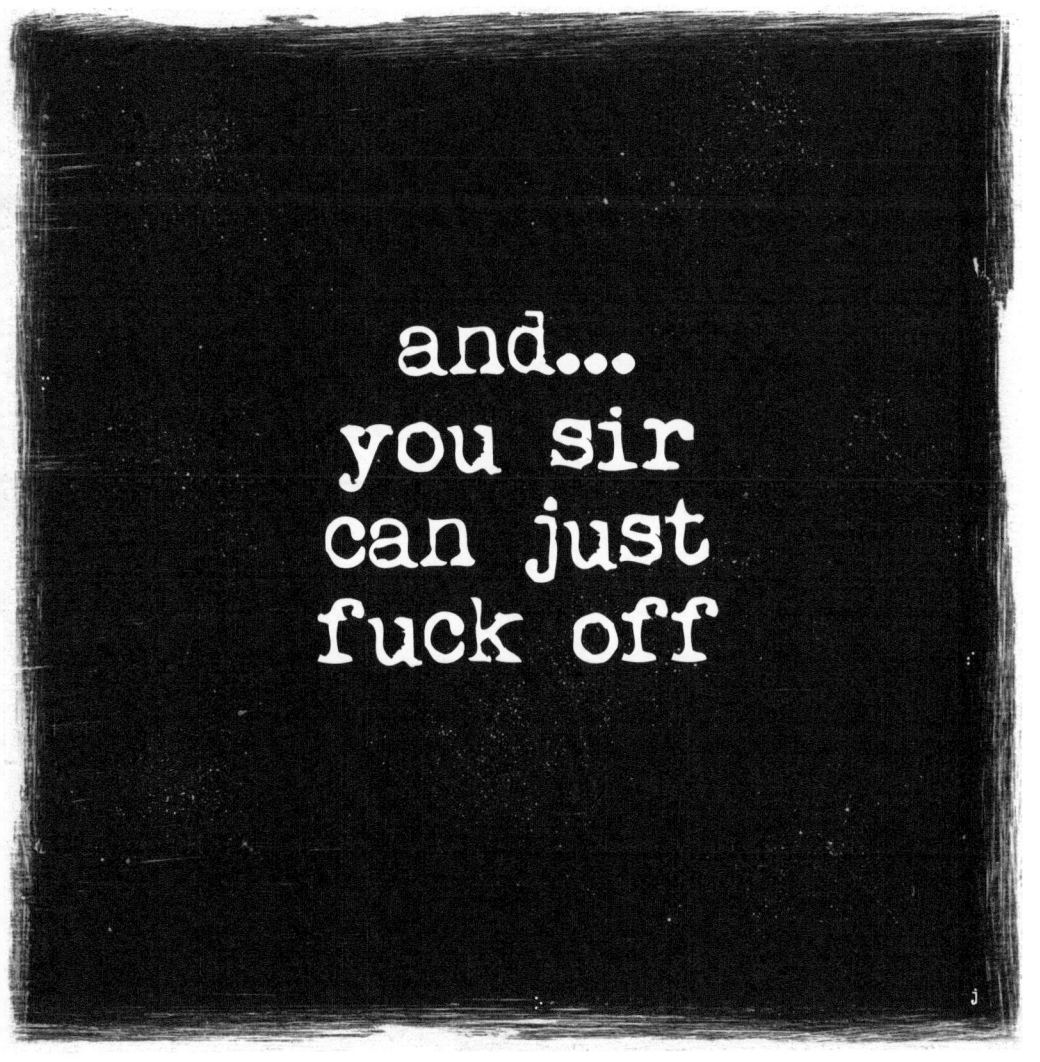

if you can't handle her flame...walk away and let someone esle enjoy the fire...

i don't date anymore...i only foster men until they find their forever homes or leave them *and sometimes...*

REALLY
GOOD
SHIT
DOES
HAPPEN...

never drink a beer
to do the job of
a shot of tequila

Don't lose sleep over someone you don't even wake up to...

the moment
you wonder
if you deserve
better...
You Do !

that look you give
someone...and think... you
are not confused...

you're a fucking idiot

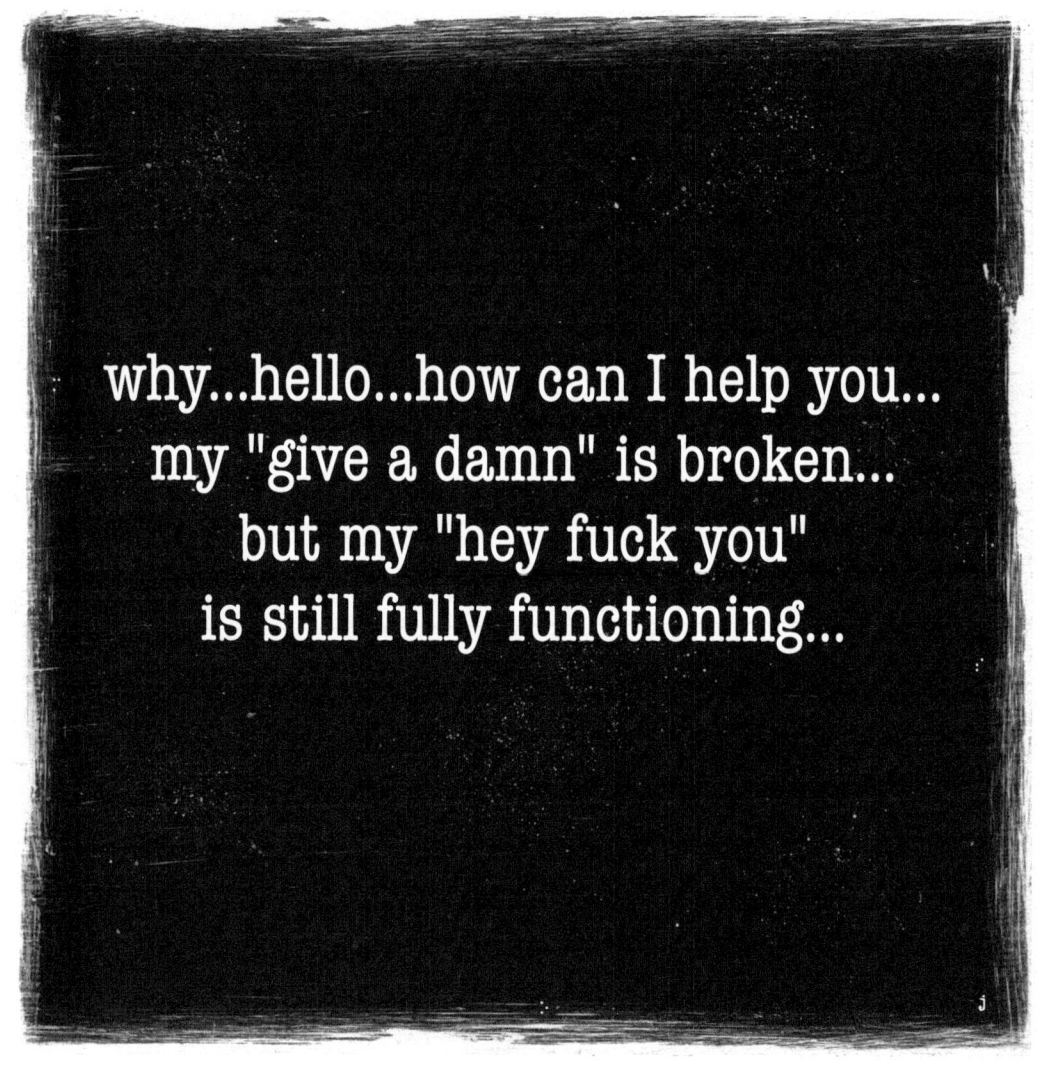

why...hello...how can I help you...
my "give a damn" is broken...
but my "hey fuck you"
is still fully functioning...

Total bullshit
Just ate a
candy bar...
and I'm still
a bitch!

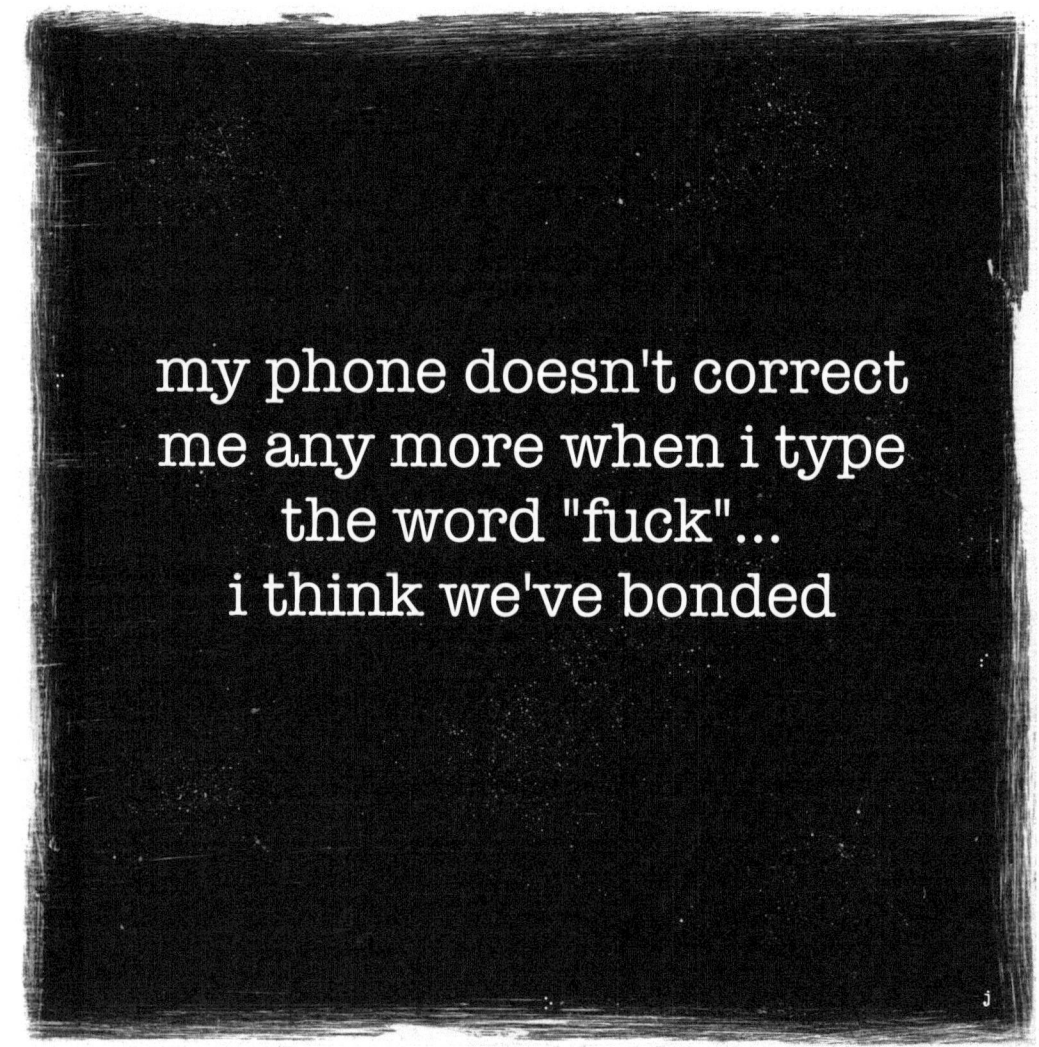

my phone doesn't correct
me any more when i type
the word "fuck"...
i think we've bonded

my wings are broken…

my halo is bent…

my horns are showing…

Yes… it's going to be one

of those days…

It costs nothing to
be kind…
sometimes just
my sanity…
but that's
nothing anymore

you're either
on my side...
by my side...
or
in my fucking way

choose wisely...

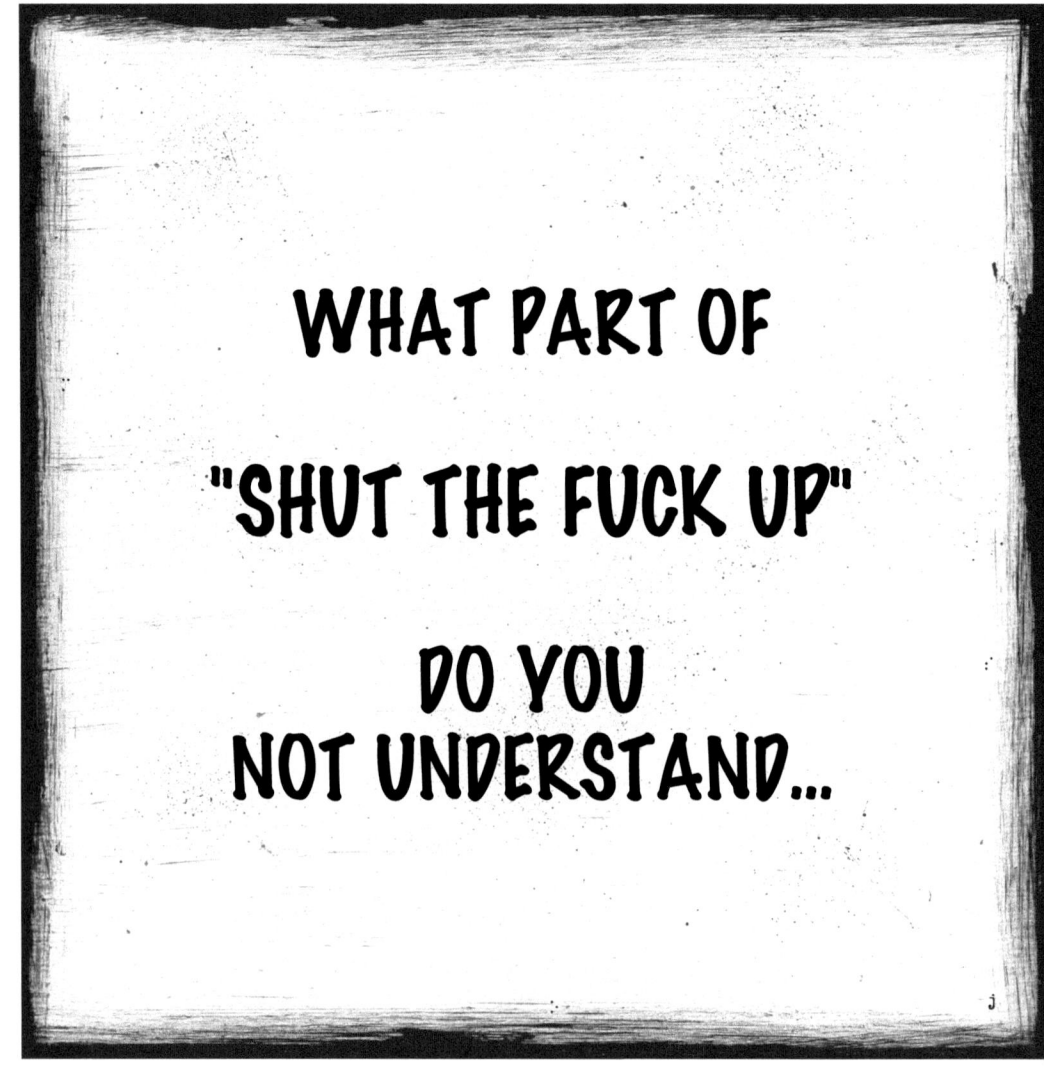

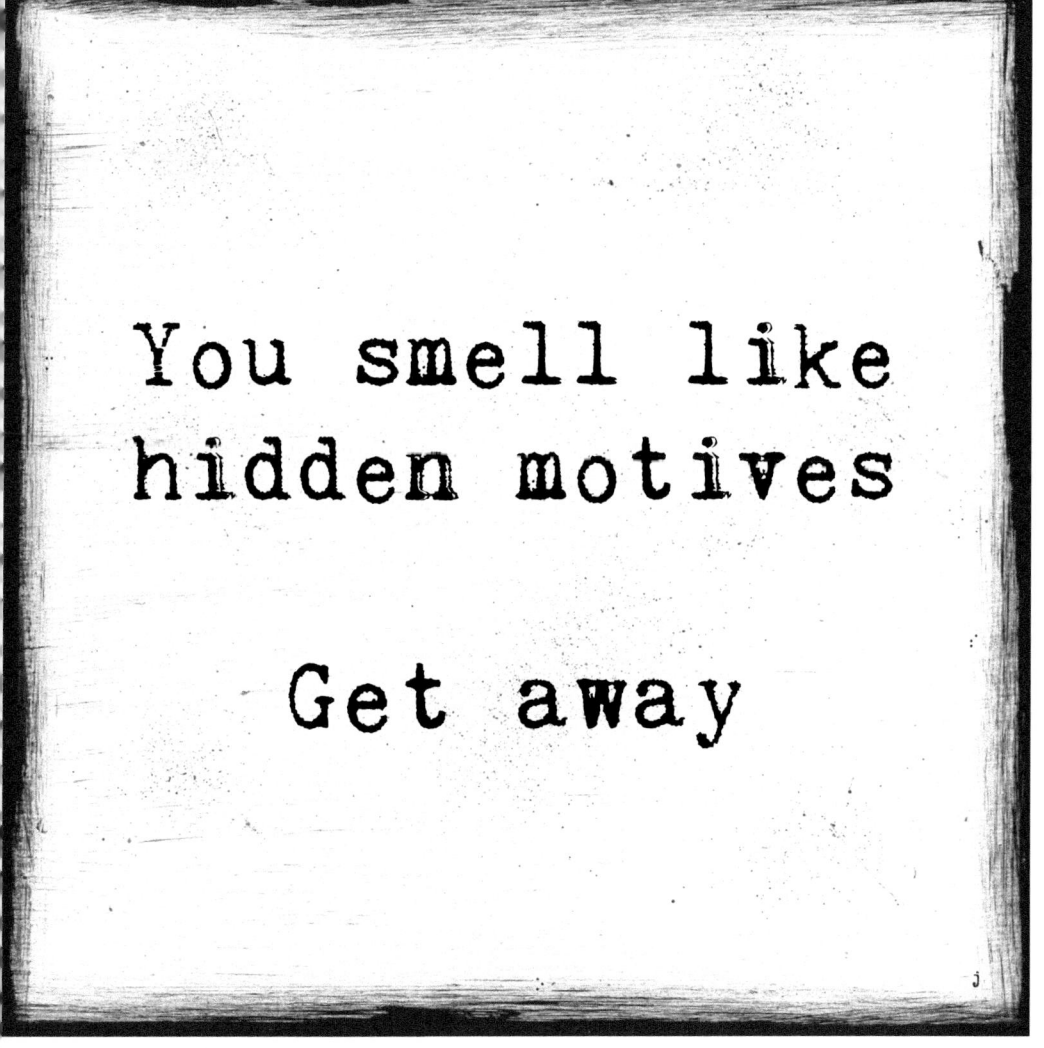

You smell like
hidden motives

Get away

it's been a beautiful day...
now watch some bitch
come along
and
fuck it up...

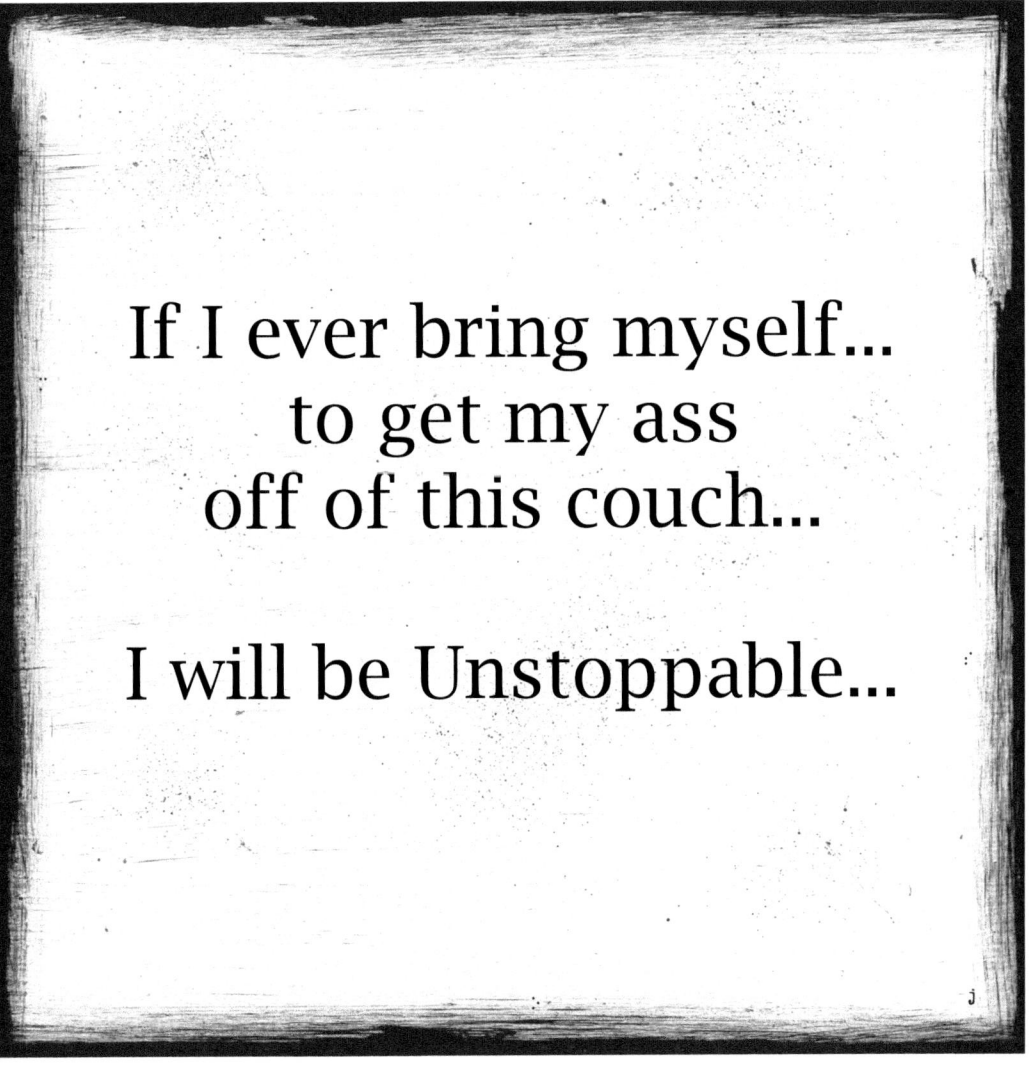

If I ever bring myself...
to get my ass
off of this couch...

I will be Unstoppable...

As a woman...I feel too
deeply and care too much...
that's what makes my
love so strong...
that's also what makes me
a real bitch
if you fuck with me.

today i'm wearing
a lovely shade of
'i slept like shit'...
so please
don't piss me off

i'm not
Perfect…and will
admit to my
mistakes…hell…
one time i even
got married

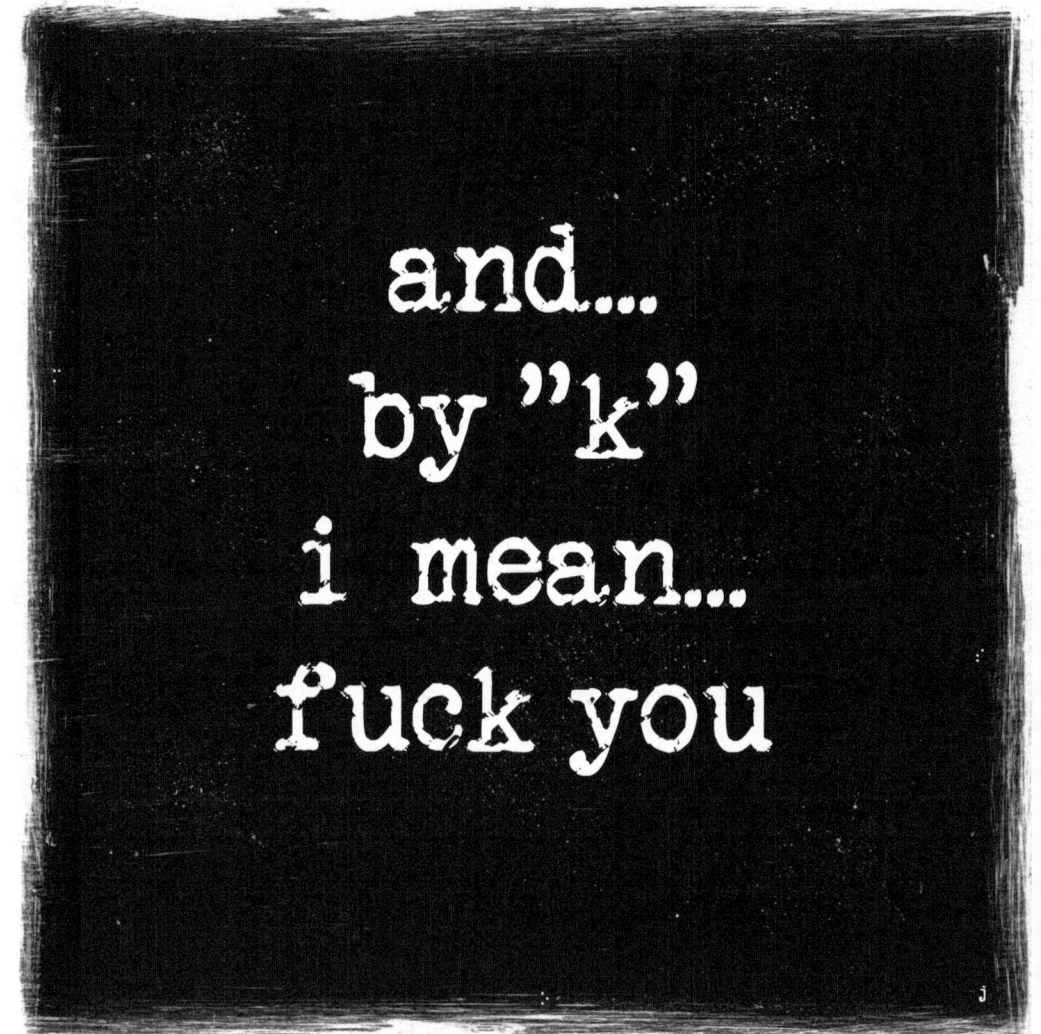

I HAVE
MULTIPLE
PERSONALITIES...
and none of them
like you...

That's how I roll...
"Lady Like "...with a wad
of "Bitch " in my
back pocket.

yes...
i've licked it...
so yes...
it's mine...

and...
oh boy...
**today's shit...
is not what
I expected.**

if we dated for less
than two months...

you were an experiment...

and yes... your dick
is too small...

AND...

NOBODY DRINKS
AN ENTIRE BOTTLE OF
ANYTHING JUST FOR FUN...

little did i
know...
we could have
more than one
midlife
crisis

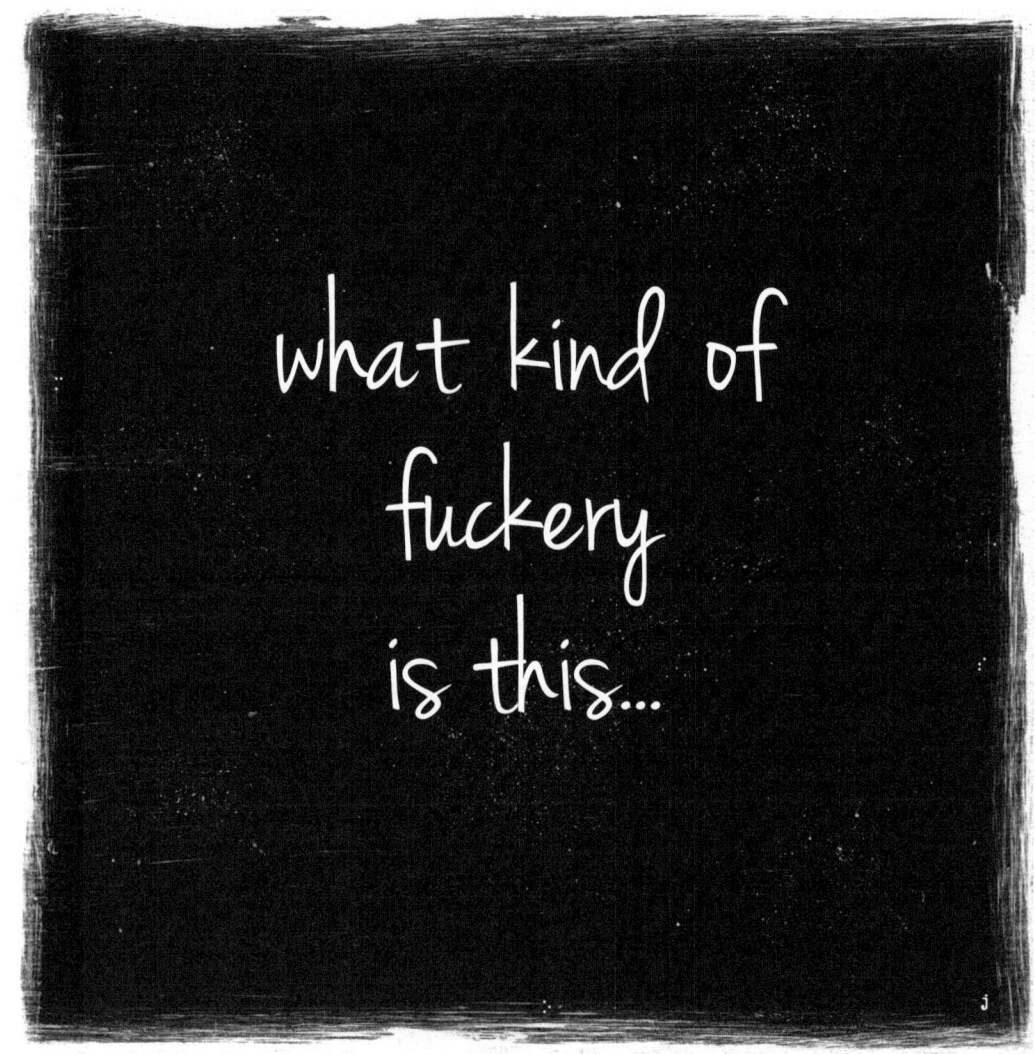

there will always be...

that little bit of...

"Fuck You"

in "Whatever"

mood enhancers...

tequila
and
a
suntan

go

Fuck

yourself

FIRST GOD CREATED
MAN...
THEN
HE REALIZED...
HE HAD...
A BETTER IDEA

Once you get
screwed over...
you stop
giving a damn
about a lot of things...

most of the time...

it takes balls
to be a woman.

To hell with
second chances...

People
never change...

This next drink may make me a tad slutty.

"As per my last email..."

Is office lingo for ...

"Bitch can you read..."

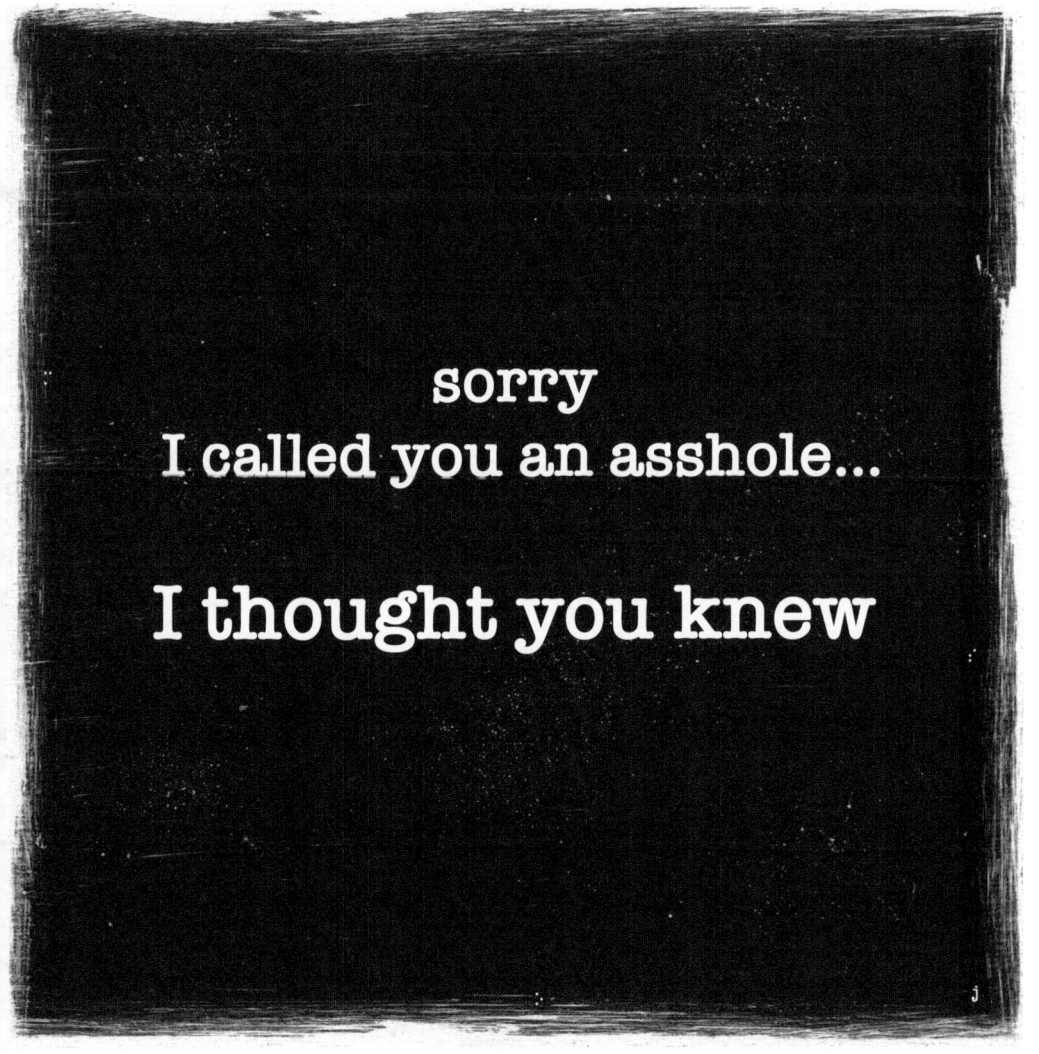

sorry
I called you an asshole...

I thought you knew

today's forecast...
Severely bitchy...
With an 100% chance
of me...telling you ...
to go eat a dick...

You can not
imagine
the immensity of
the Damns...
I do not Give...

I typed "bitch" into my GPS... and guess who's driveway I'm in...

Judging my choices would be a complete waste of your time... I've already done that...and rationalized them too...

go ahead...
do something you probably shouldn't
you know... add some spice...
to your already fucked up life...

BECAUSE
I SAID SO
THAT'S
WHY

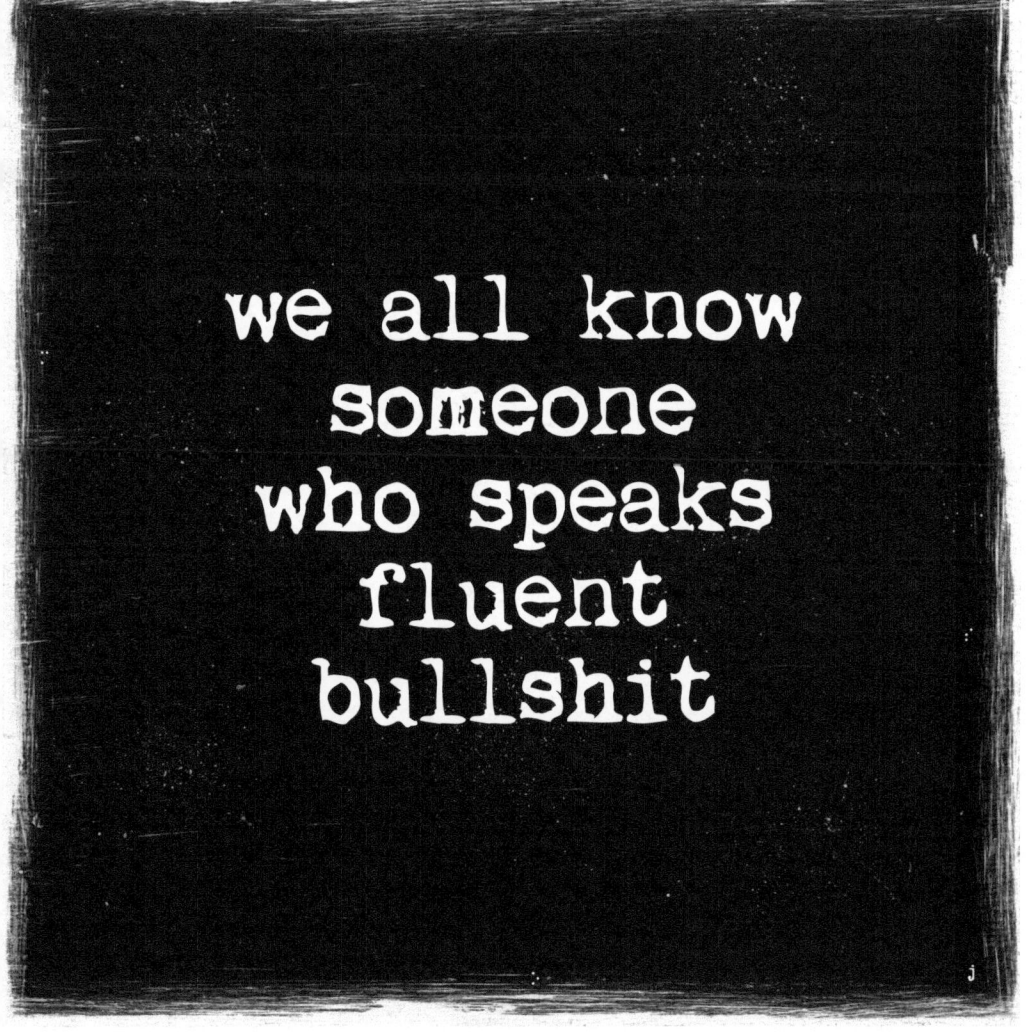

we all know
someone
who speaks
fluent
bullshit

When I'm drunk...
"Drinks for everyone"

When I'm sober...
"$5 for shipping? Hard no."

almost every hand
you have ever
shaken...
has had a dick
in it

and...
then there's those
that always say you
can count on them...
but you know not
to hold your breath
waiting for them...

no...
fuck you.

you broke my heart...

and...that look
on your face
says...I will be
needing a
drink...

and... that would
be the 'thing'
your Mother warned
you about...

things have
changed...
I no longer
give a
damn...

this
is
my
therapy...
fuck off

sorry for the mean...
awful... but accurate
things i've said...

Of course I speak
my mind...
My head would
explode...
if I kept all this
BITCHING to myself

Then...
you realize...
Your
Happily
Ever After...
doesn't include
"that"anymore

most of the time...
i don't give a fuck...

what

is

your

superpower?

Oh honey...
You think
you're the
only one...

if you show me you don't
give a damn...

i will show you...
i'm better at it

starting to
get that
"nope"
attitude
about
everything...

If I walk into the room without pants...

yes... it means you're staying

tired of getting

my hopes up

for nothing...

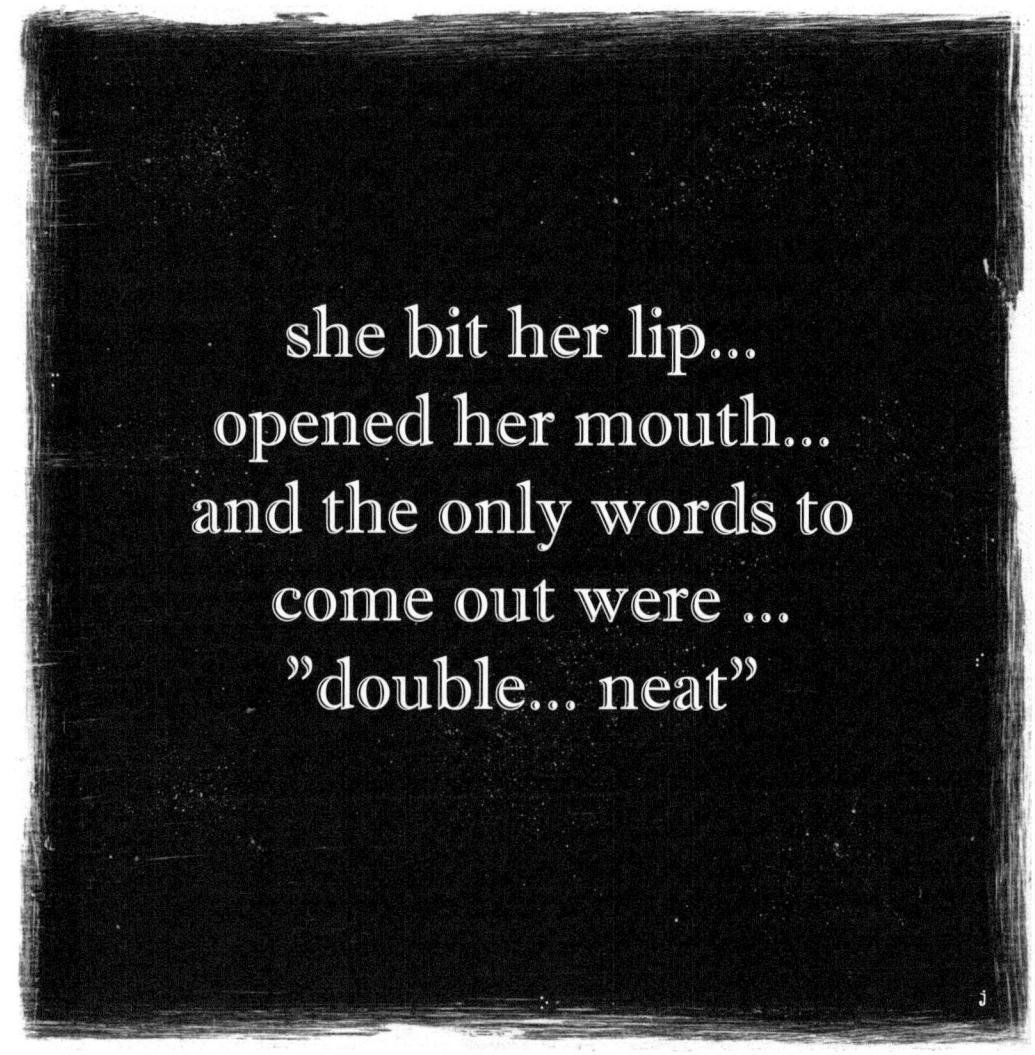

she bit her lip...
opened her mouth...
and the only words to
come out were ...
"double... neat"

my
bitch face
doesn't
rest
anymore

J

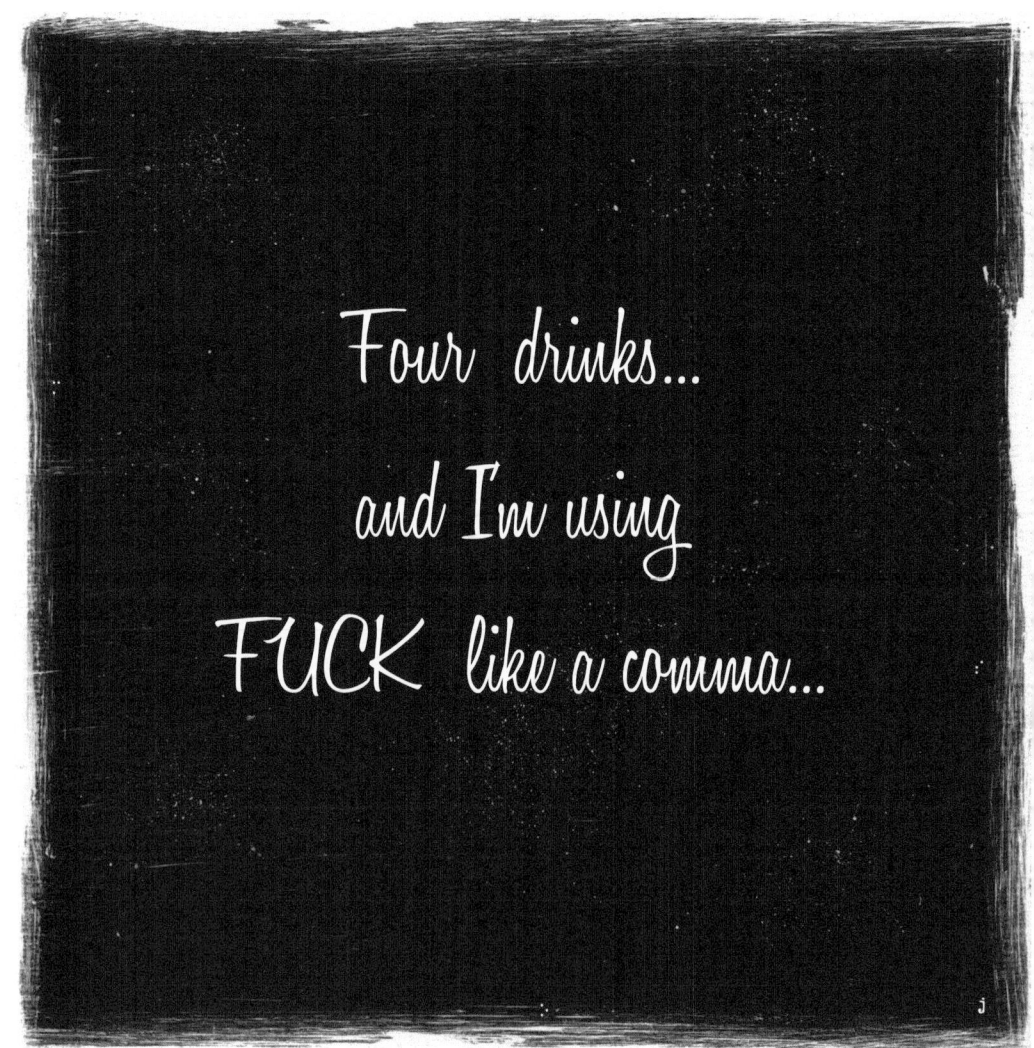

215

is there a level beyond
"craziest bitch ever"...
I'd hate to think
she has plateaued...

Absofuckinlutely

you seem confused...

the people who give
a damn...
are right
over there...

some people are
just beautifully
wrapped...
pieces of shit

Hello...
looking to buy a car...
does a dickhead
named Vinny
work here...

220

DON'T
BE
A
DICK

just...
fuck me

I'm a
happy-go-lucky
ray of
fucking
sunshine.

and...
bitch...
believe
in
something...

and...some days...
it's just best
to
watch...

not only does
my mind
wander...

sometimes it
fucks off completely...

GET DRUNK...

I NEED
THE
TRUTH

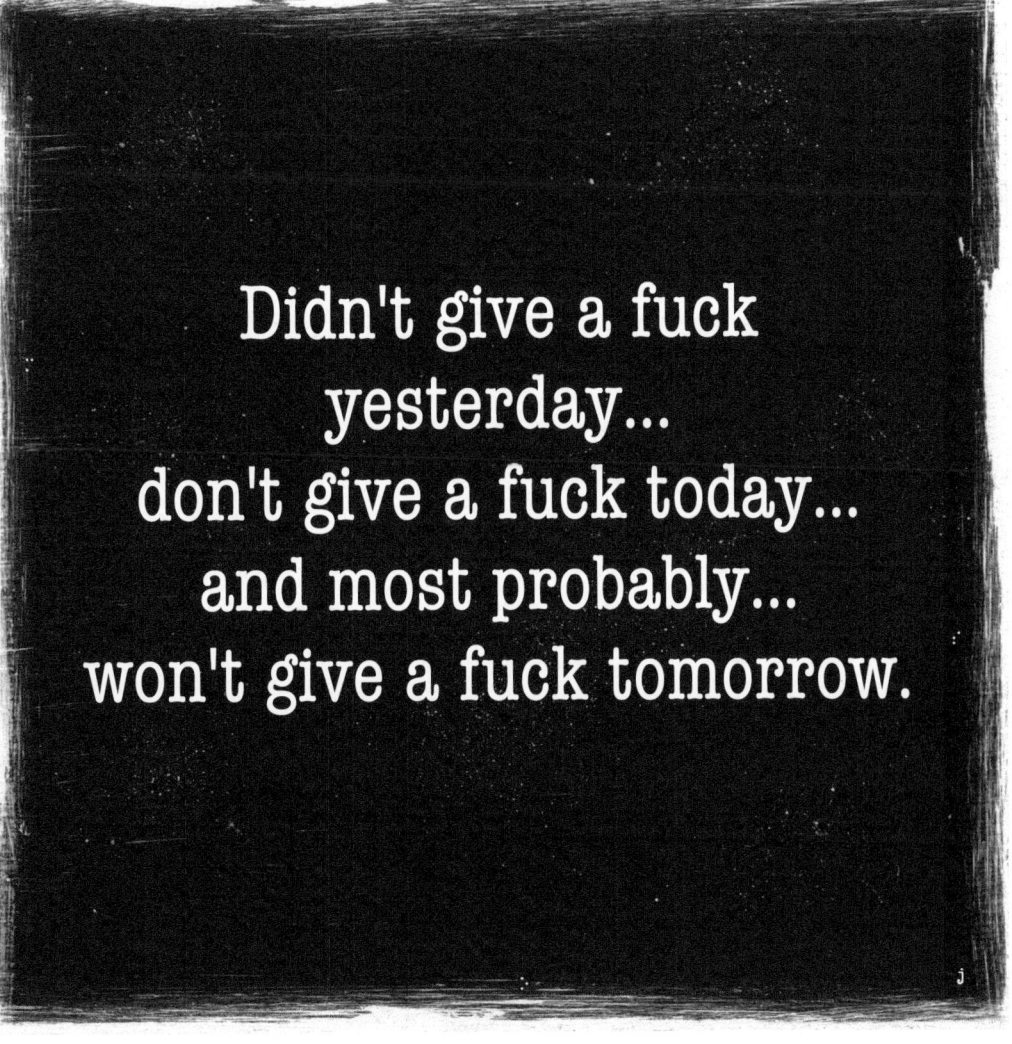

Didn't give a fuck
yesterday...
don't give a fuck today...
and most probably...
won't give a fuck tomorrow.

Surround yourself
with people who
actually get it...

The whiskey
still works... It
just depends on
what it's for...
and who you are
with

and...
then you realize
things will never be
as you wish because
you are a decent human
being with a handful
of scruples

then i said
goodnight...tucked you
away inside a place
called nostalgia...
where you'll
always remain

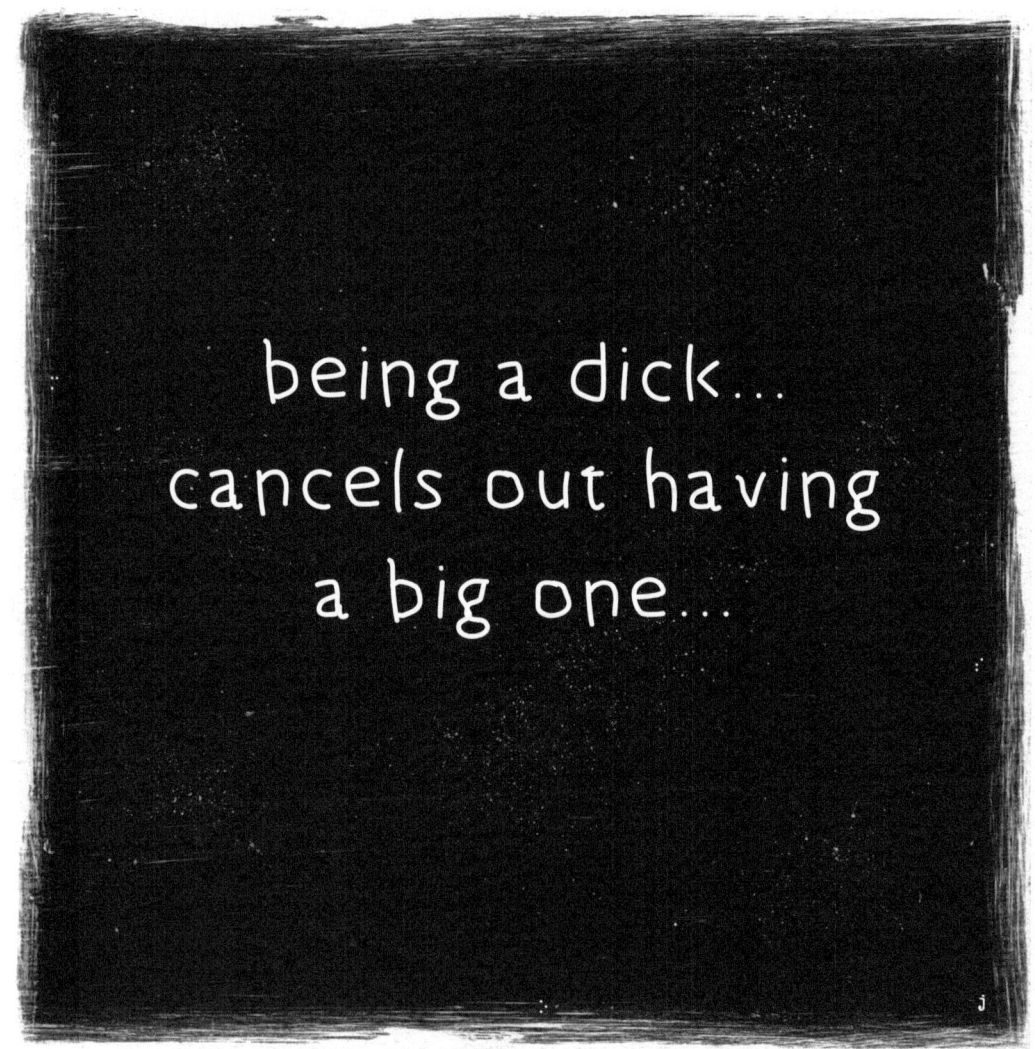

being a dick...
cancels out having
a big one...

who left

the bag of

fuckin'

idiots open

i don't pretend to be anything i'm not...

except for sober...
i've pretended to be sober
a few times

why
are all
great changes

preceded
by
chaos

and today...
I will do absolutely
fucking NOTHING

Then you're half
way into a two
week notice...
and you really
don't give a shit

as long as
everything is exactly
the way I want...

I'm totally fucking
flexible...

and...
most days you
will have
to create
your own damn
sunshine

ON THE MENU
FOR TODAY...
UNPRODUCTIVE...WITH A SIDE
OF DICKING AROUND...

i hate when the
light at the end of
the tunnel...
is a damn train

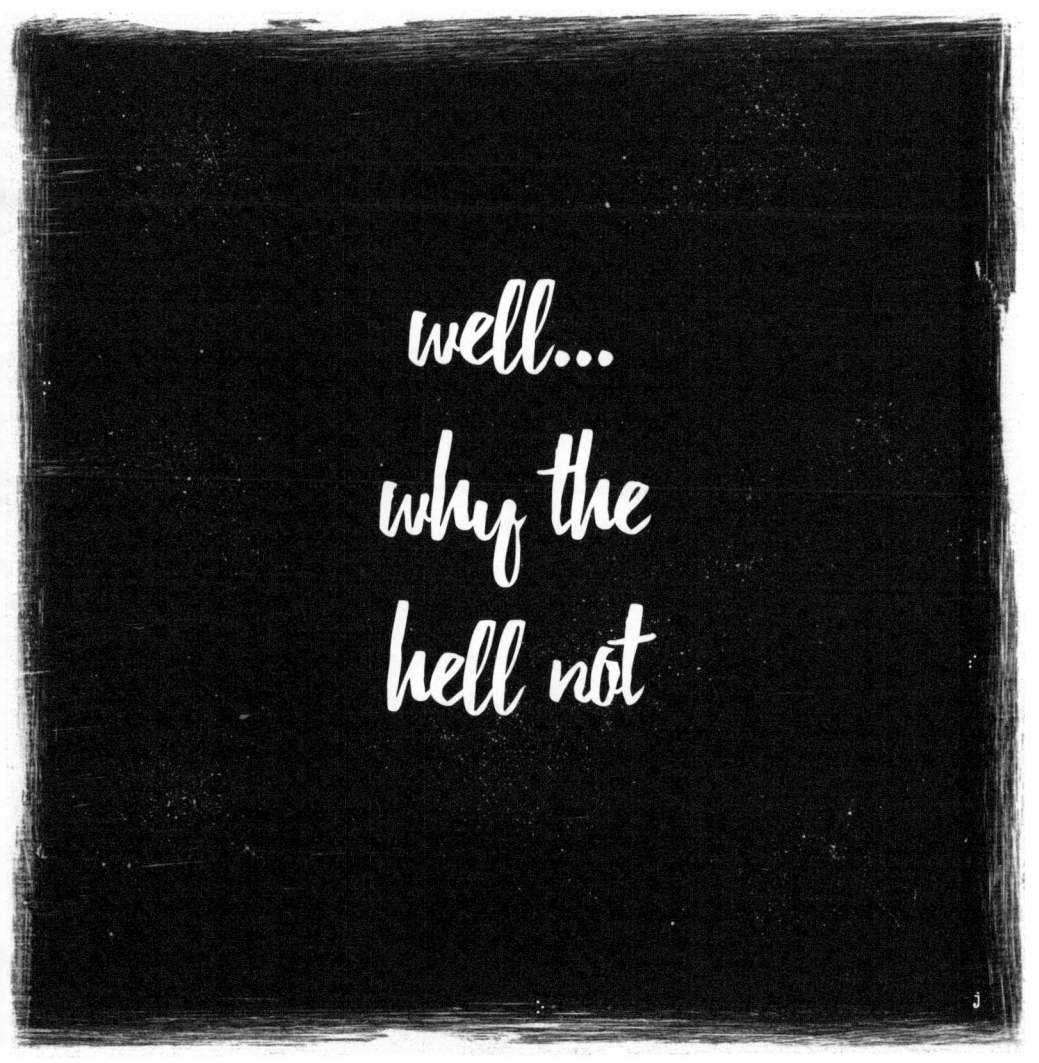

I express all of my
emotions by saying...
"fuck" in varying tones.

you call me
a bitch
like it's
a bad thing

they say it's
what's on the inside
that counts...
i agree...
but i'm keeping my
DAMN hair appointment
just in case...

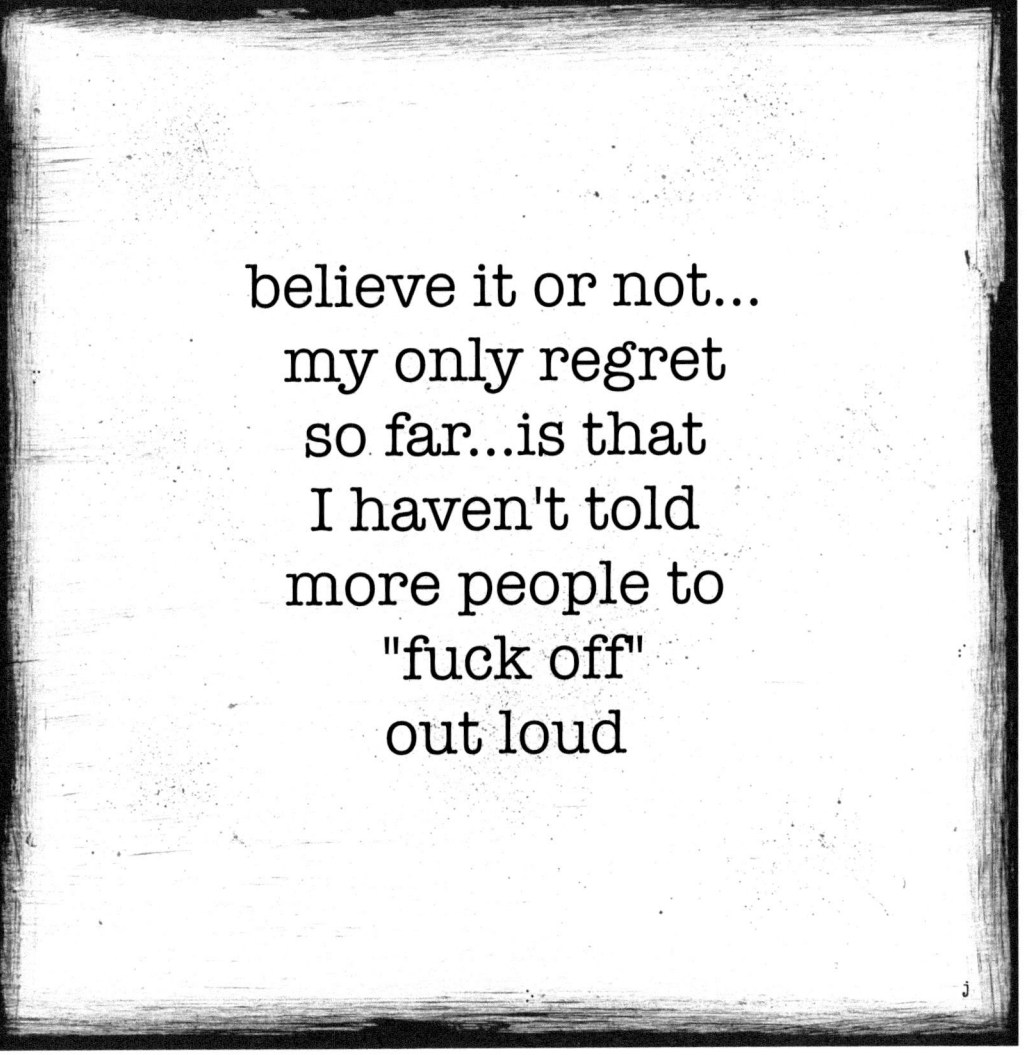

believe it or not...
my only regret
so far...is that
I haven't told
more people to
"fuck off"
out loud

and...
your panties...
will reflect
your intentions...

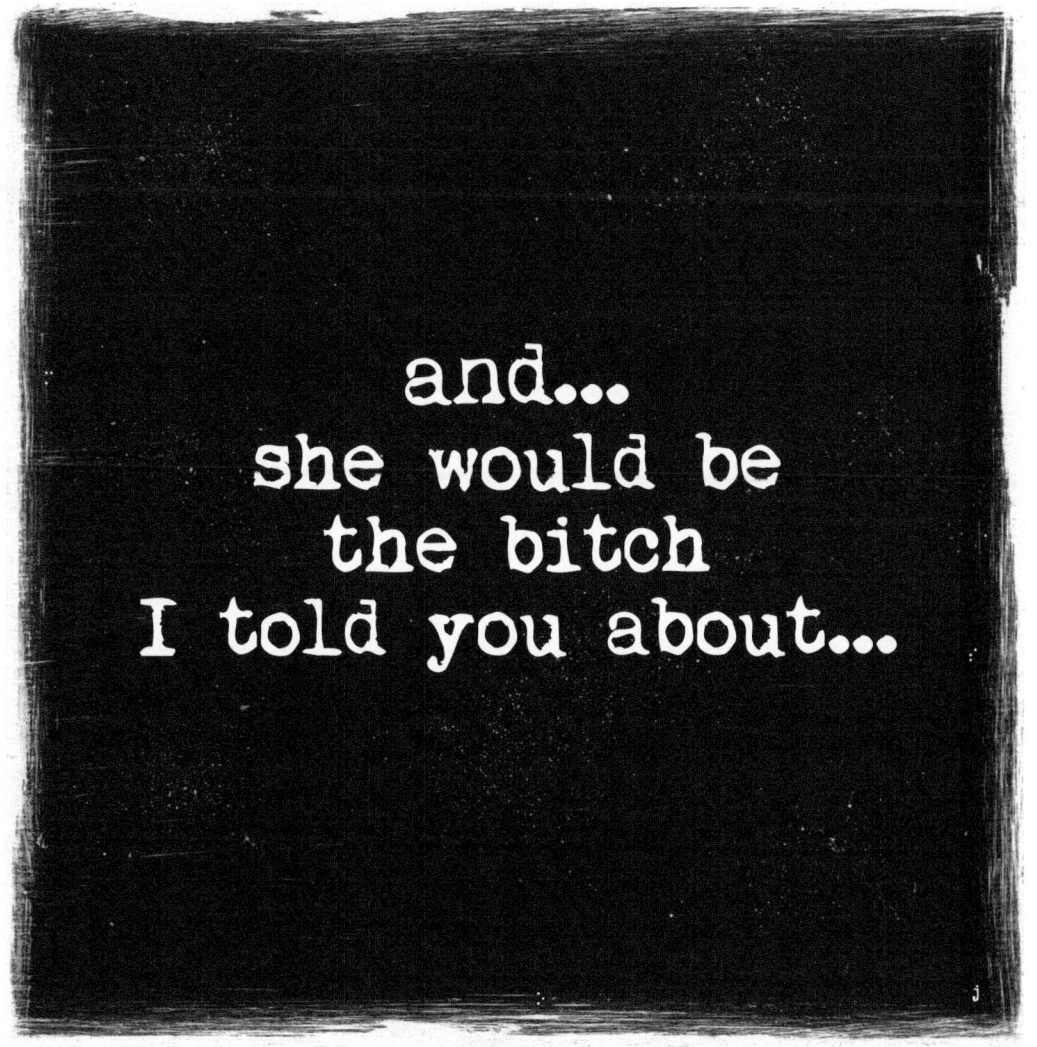

and...
she would be
the bitch
I told you about...

just
chuck it
in the "fuck it"
bucket
and move on

Karma...
is a good judge of character...

you...my friend... are fucked.

3 rules for life...

1. fuck
2. dont give a fuck
3. don't get fucked over

i'm a sweet
girl...but if you
piss me off...
i have a pocket
full of crazy
just waitin'
to come out

i'm trying not to
use the "f word"
so much...

but it's proving to be
'hucking' hard...

do not judge the
story
by the
'hucking' chapter
you walked in on

Your lack
of
swearing...
makes my ass
uncomfortable

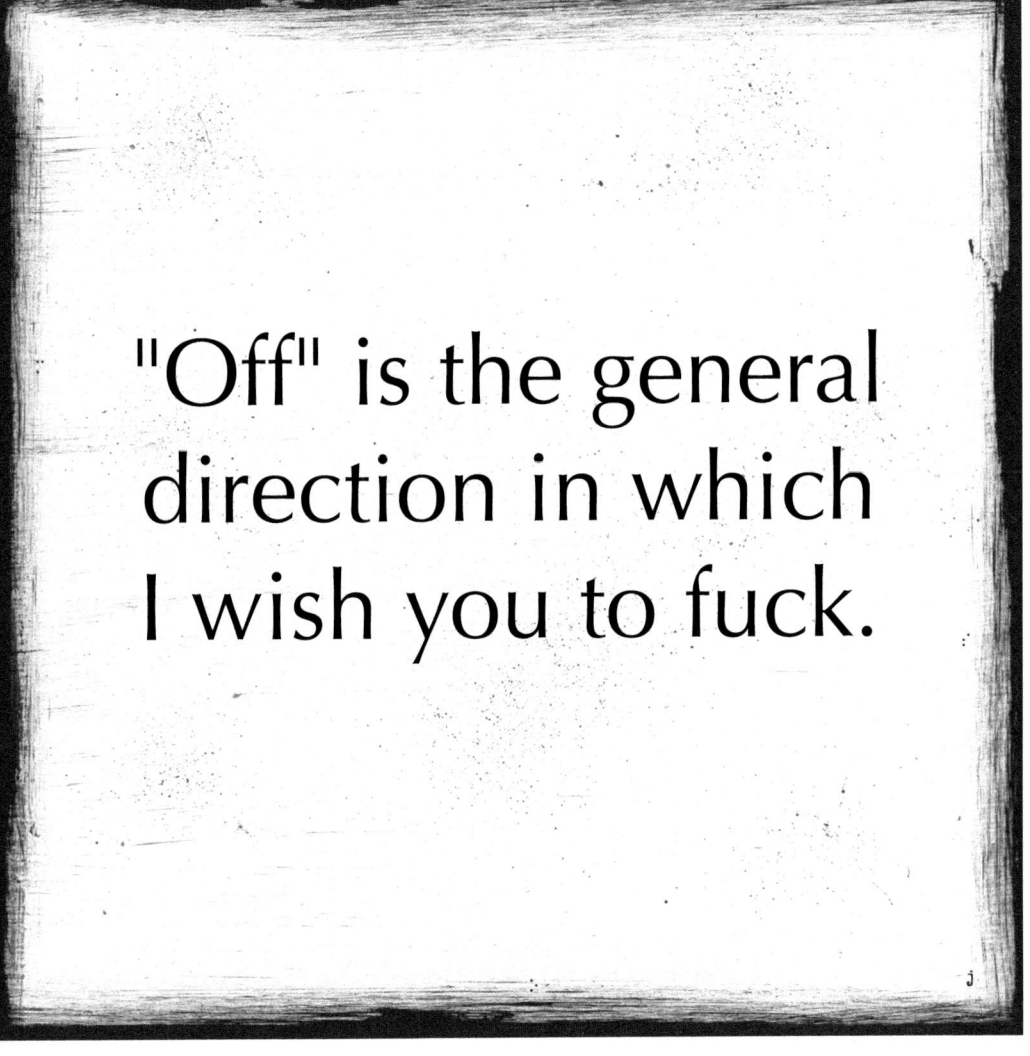

"Off" is the general direction in which I wish you to fuck.

everything happens for
a reason...
except for the things
you fuck up
by yourself...

I like what I do...
and do what I like...
and in no particular
order

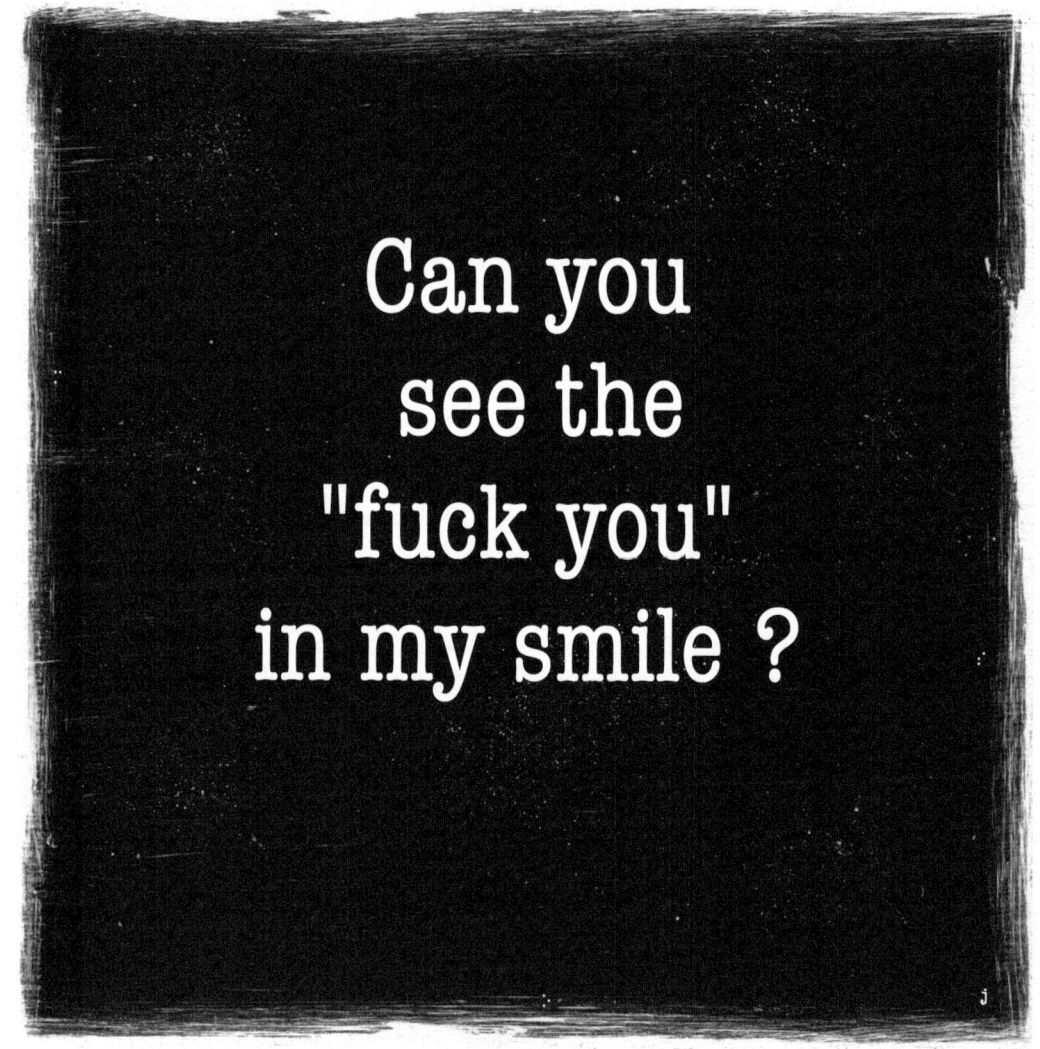

Behind every
'bad bitch' is a
sweet girl who
got tired of
everyone's
bullshit

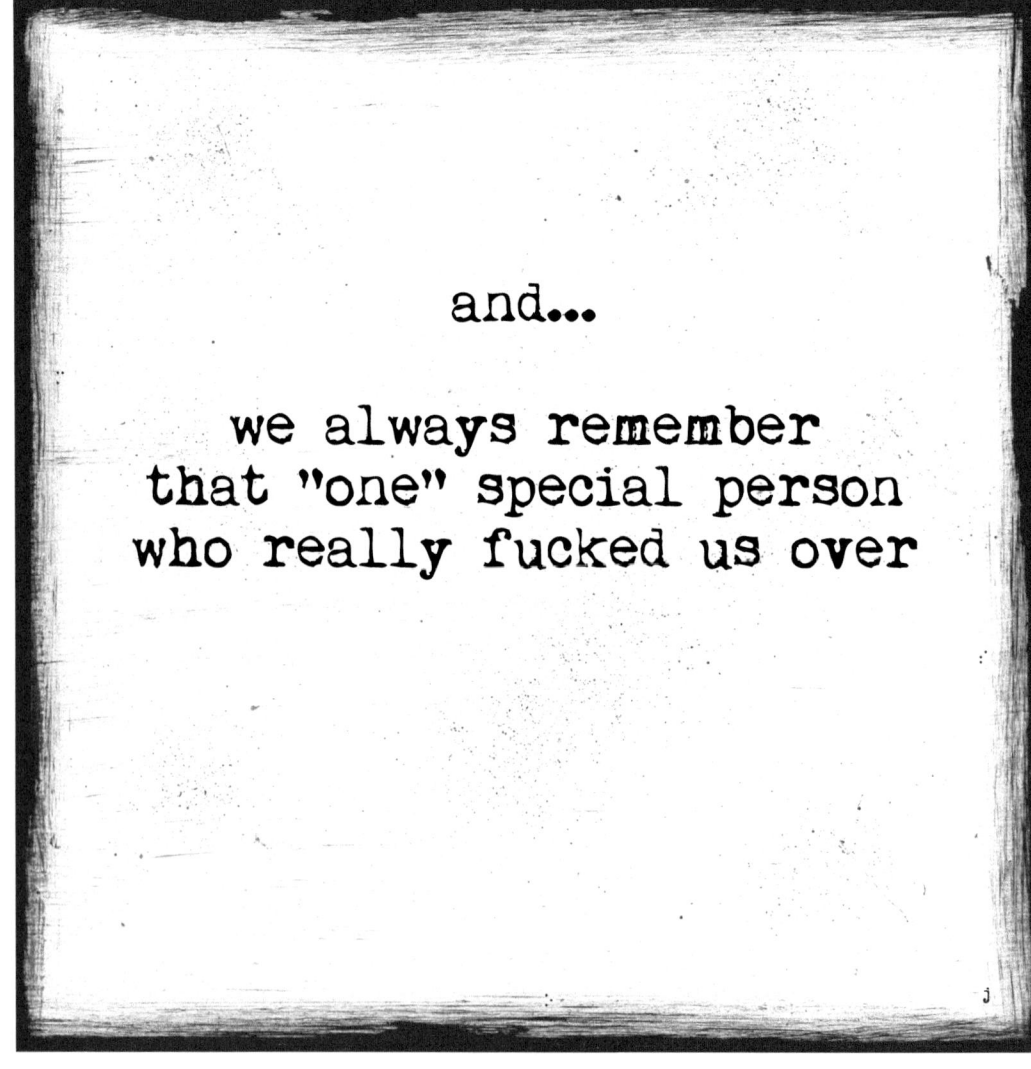

and...

we always remember
that "one" special person
who really fucked us over

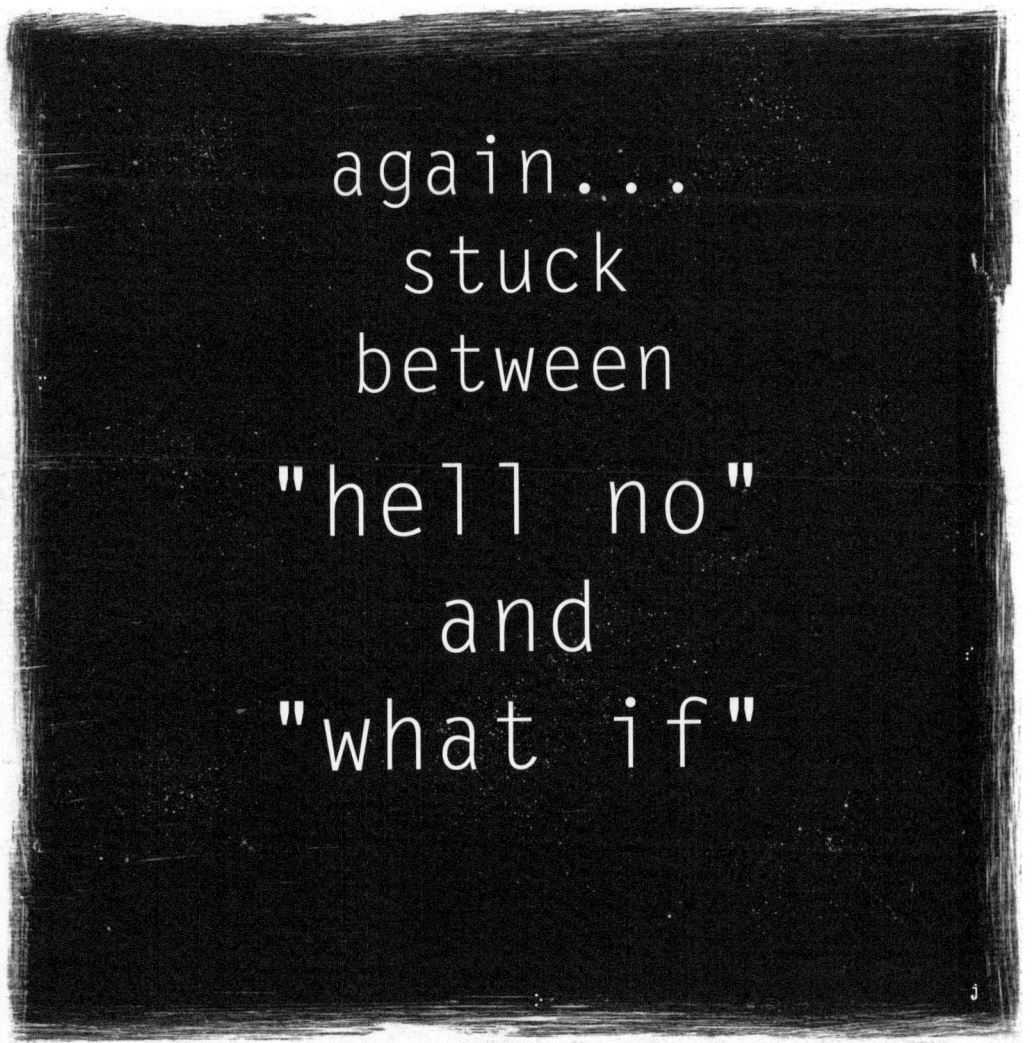

again...
stuck
between
"hell no"
and
"what if"

keeping
calm...
just doesn't
suit me

Mom...
I have
a paper cut...

Cool...
you weighed 9
pounds at birth

is everything
expensive...
or
am i just
FUCKING
POOR

Pulling the
"crazy" card

has helped me
through a LOT
of situations

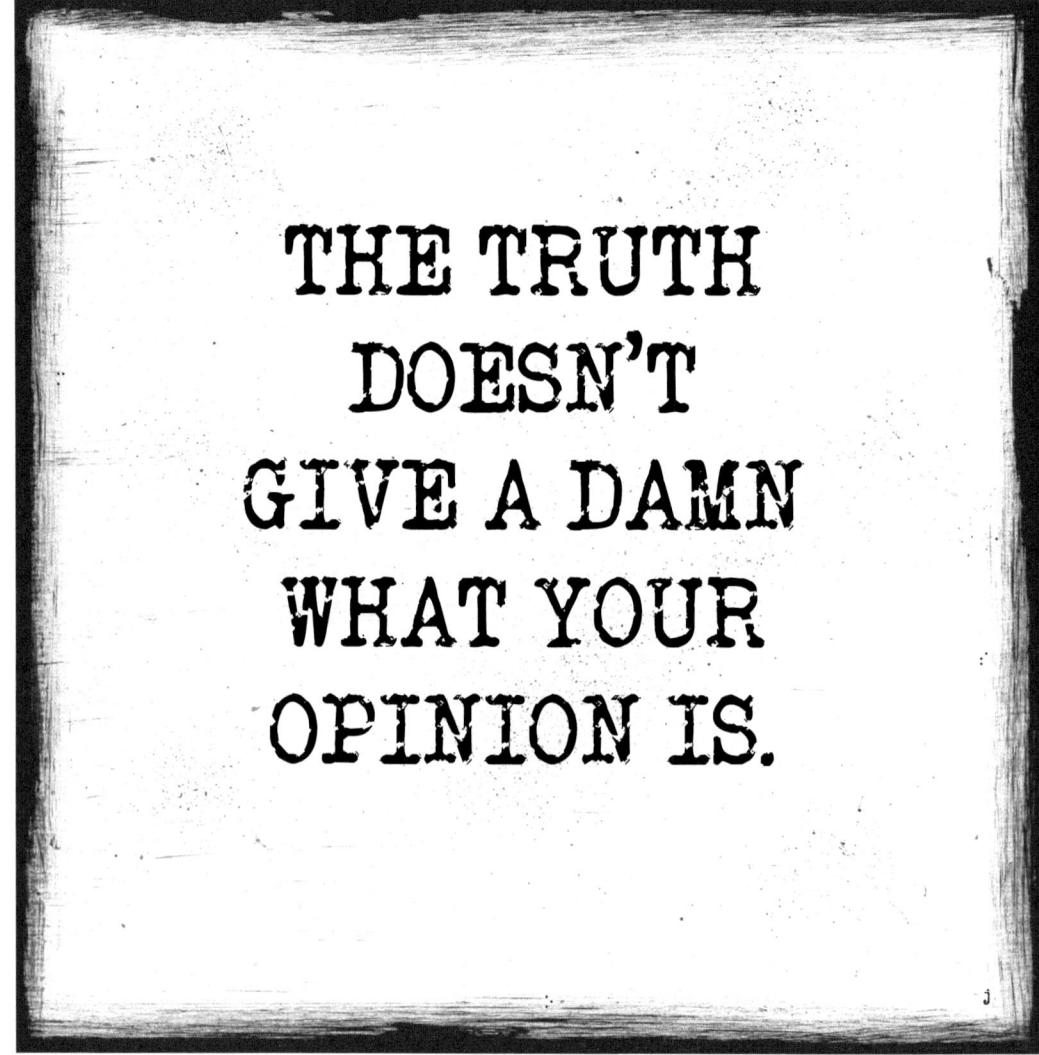

THE TRUTH
DOESN'T
GIVE A DAMN
WHAT YOUR
OPINION IS.

And...
yes...
I'm still
a fucking
delight.

then there comes
that point...
where you
ultimately
don't care
any more

when you look at someone...
and finally say...

YOU
FUCKING
IDIOT

yet...
another
fucking
idiot

So tired of always pleasing the wrong one...

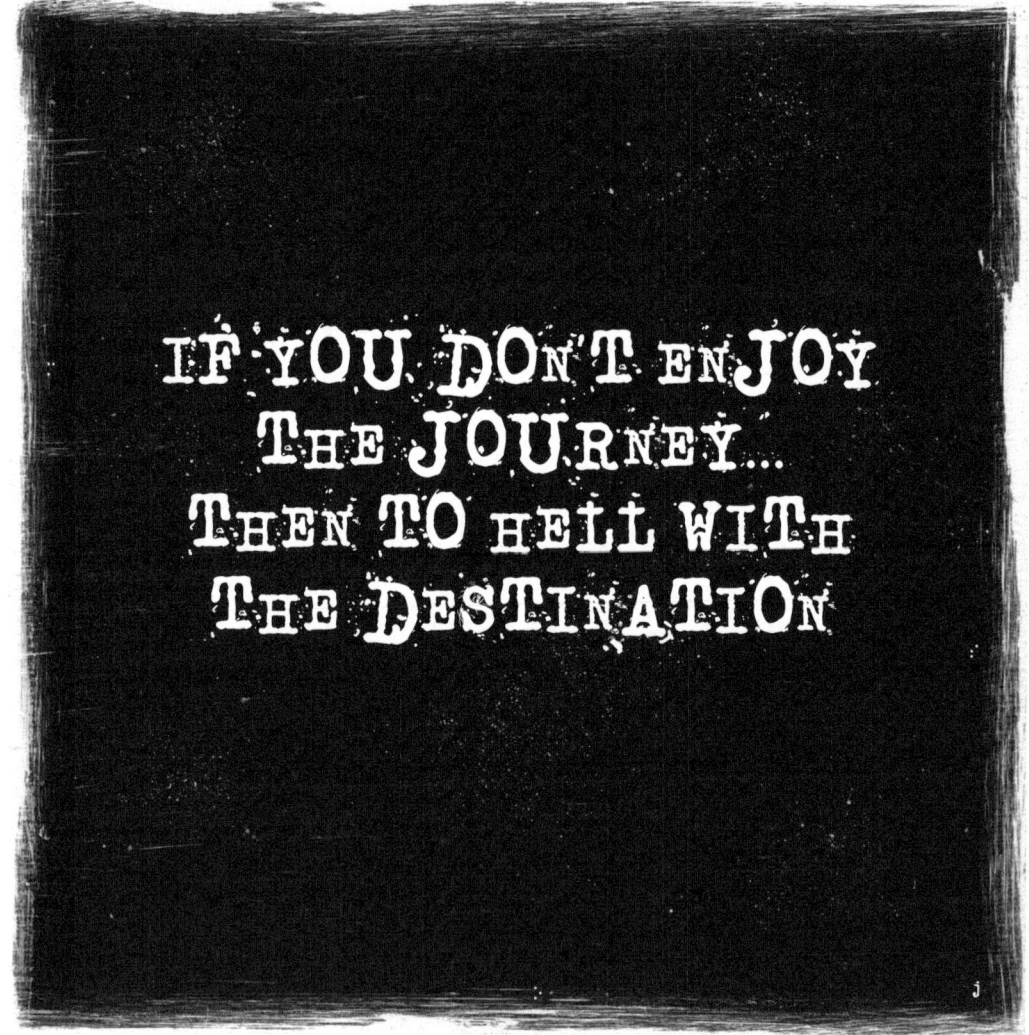

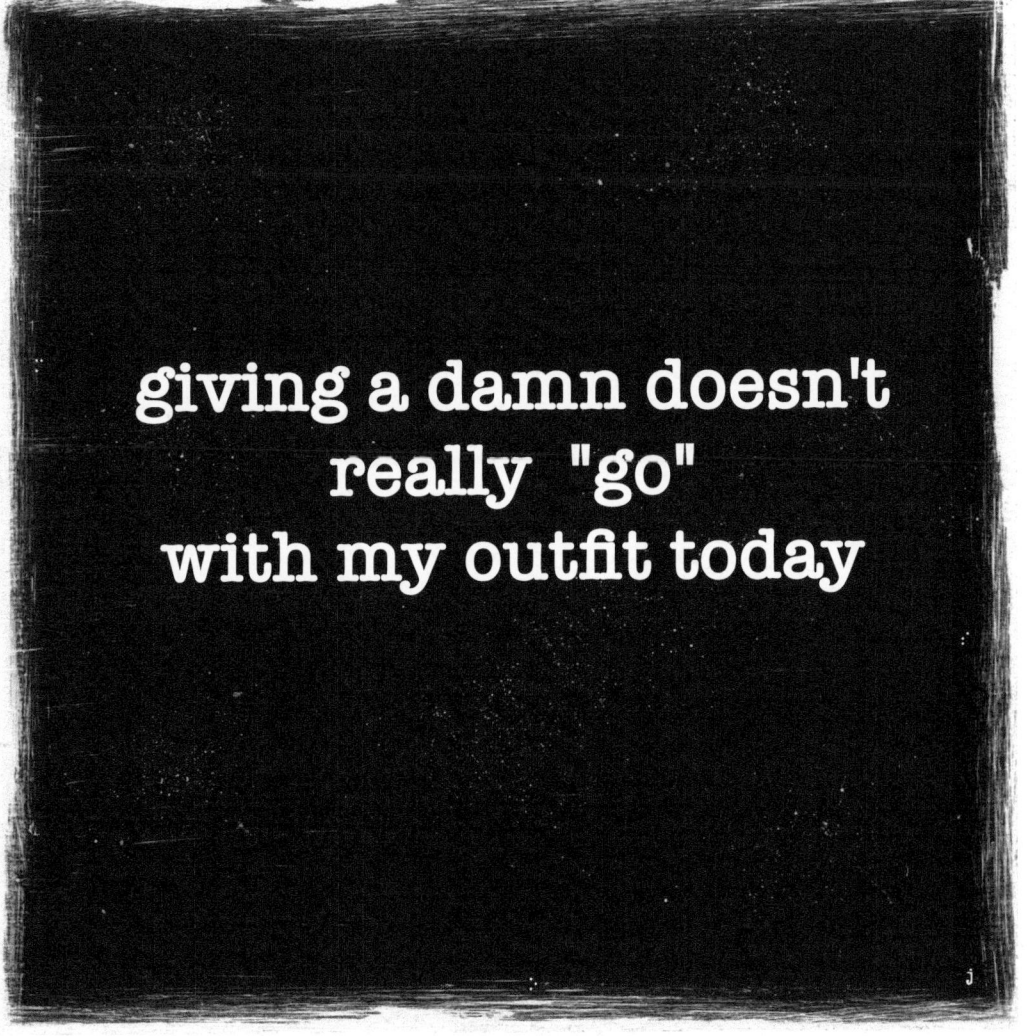

giving a damn doesn't
really "go"
with my outfit today

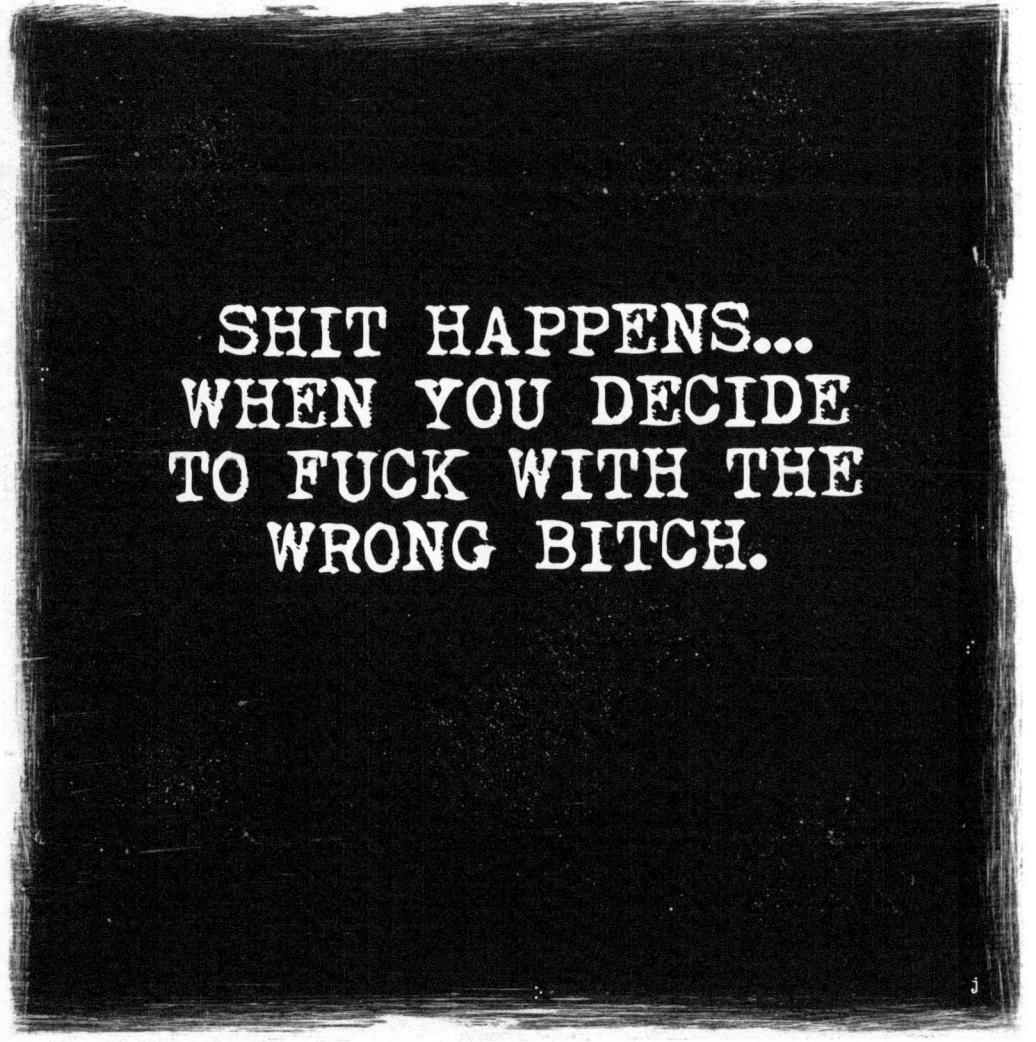

SHIT HAPPENS...
WHEN YOU DECIDE
TO FUCK WITH THE
WRONG BITCH.

"they" say swearing
is due to limited vocabulary...
I know a perpetuitous amount
of words...
but I still prefer...

"fuck off"
to
"go away"

let me adjust

my crown…and get

this f'n day started

four special moods...

i'm too old for this shit

i"m too tired for this shit

i'm too sober for this shit

and...

i don't have time for this shit

I'm a polite Bitch

I will tell
you 'Excuse Me'
and...
'Shut the Fuck up'
in the same breath

if you don't
like me...
and still watch
everything I
do...
you Bitch...
are a fan...

A shoutout to all the women who compliment other women... and actually mean it.

you know you're with
the right person
when all you have to
do is be you...

EVEN AT MY WORST...

I AM FUCKING
INCREDIBLE

Karma...

Serving up Justice...
one Asshole at a time

287

and...
I'm not the
person you
put on
speakerphone

fuck you...

i'm perfect

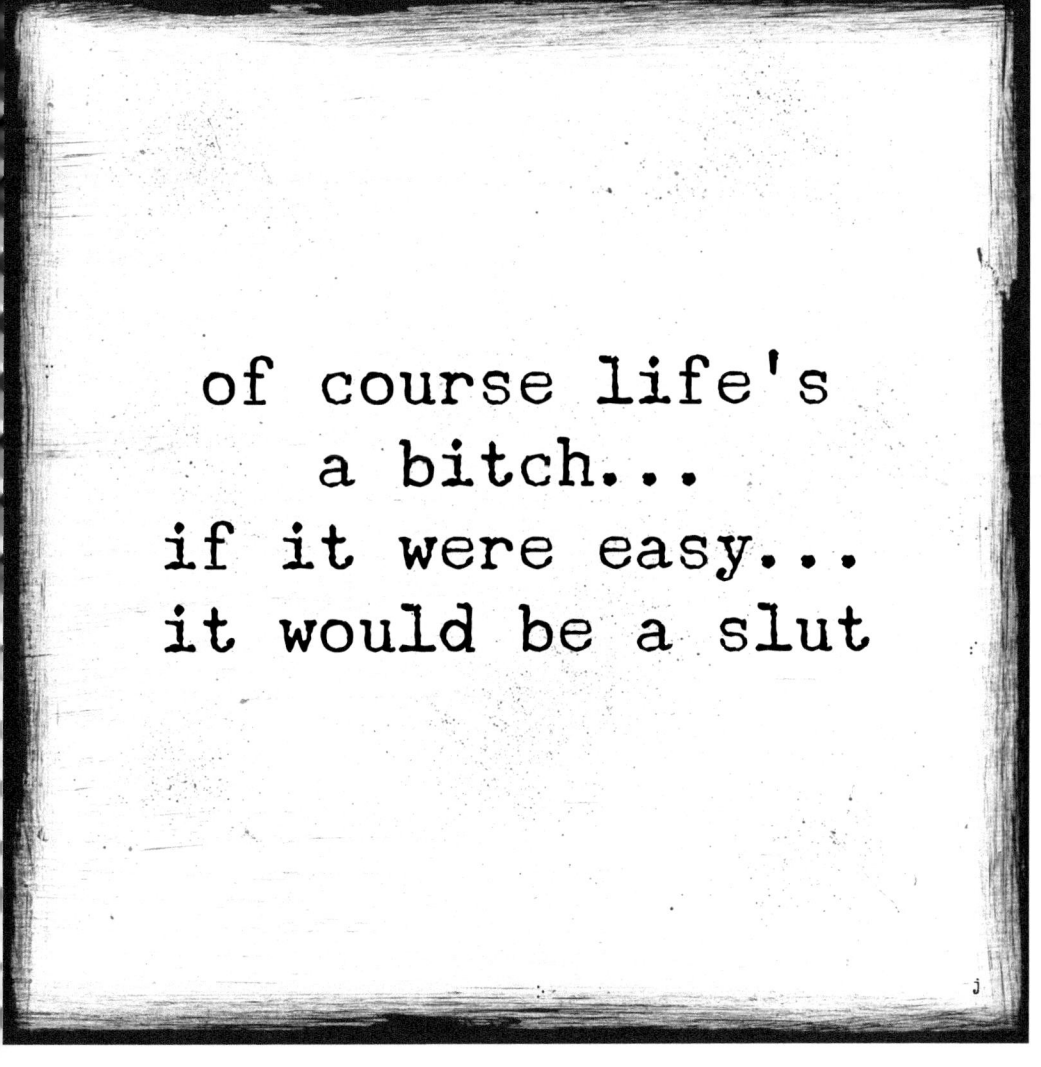

of course life's
a bitch...
if it were easy...
it would be a slut

as for my girls...
they will be raised to
breathe fire...

you really
can do
whatever
the fuck
you want

The cost of not following your heart...
is spending the rest of your life wishing you had.

One day...
some man is going to
see me chug my Long
Island Iced tea in less
than 5 seconds...
and think...
"yes... she's the one"

Unfuckwithable...

(adj.) when you're truly at peace and in touch with yourself...and nothing anyone says or does bothers you... and no negativity or drama can touch you.

... you know it's going to be a great story... when it starts out... "so there's this BITCH"...

some days...
just
dwell
in the
fuckin'
possibility

RULE # 1

There are no
fucking rules.

nothing worse
than knowing...
it's the beginning of
the end...

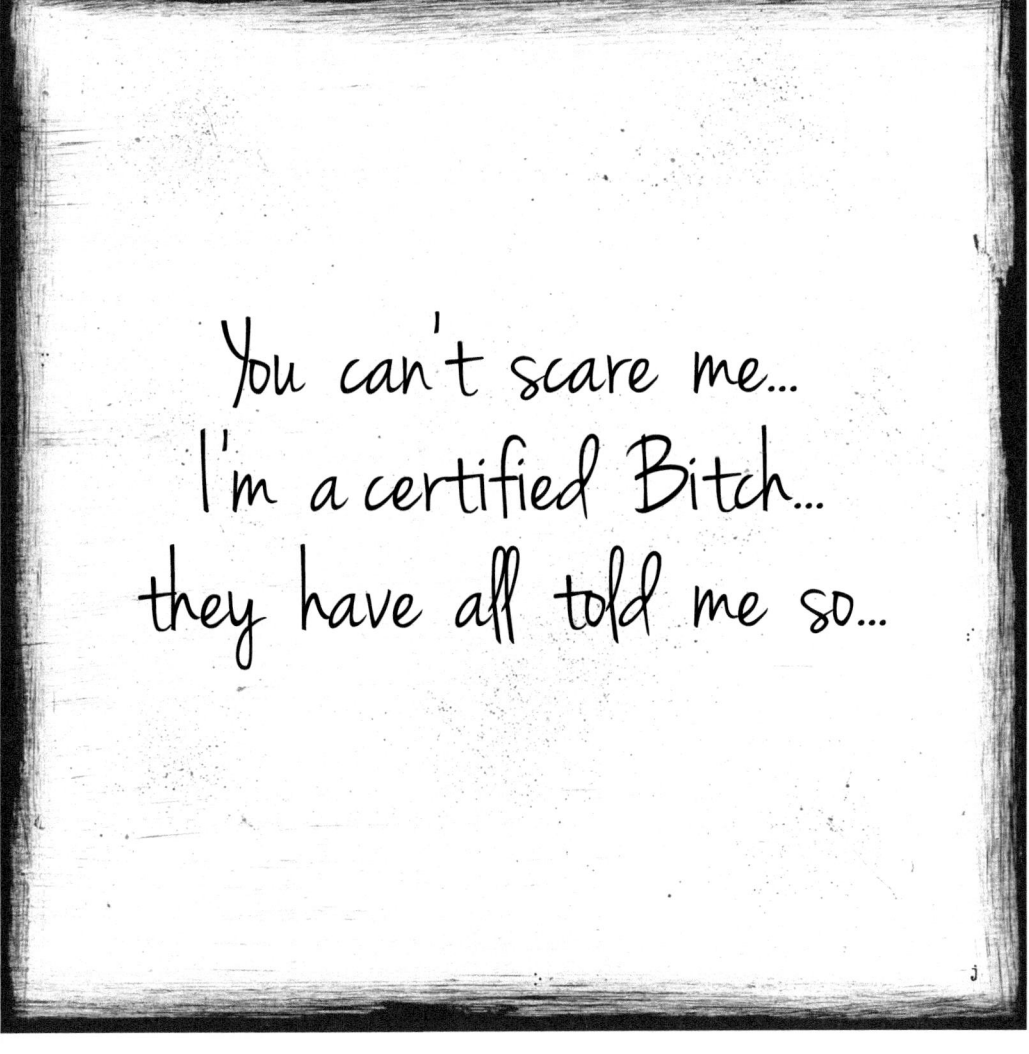

You can't scare me...
I'm a certified Bitch...
they have all told me so...

NOT EVERYONE YOU
LOSE IS A LOSS...

UNLESS IT'S ME...
THEN YOU REALLY
FUCKED UP.

on particulary
rough days when i'm
sure i can't endure
much more... i remind
myself...my track record
for getting through
bad days has been
one hundred percent...
so i will shine on

my boss said i
intimidate co
workers...i
just stared at
him until he
apologized

you Had me
at...
"today I Hate
PeoPie"

Your constructive
criticism has been noted...
and is appreciated...
now...
fuck you very much.

She became dangerous
to them when she no
longer needed or cared for
their approval...

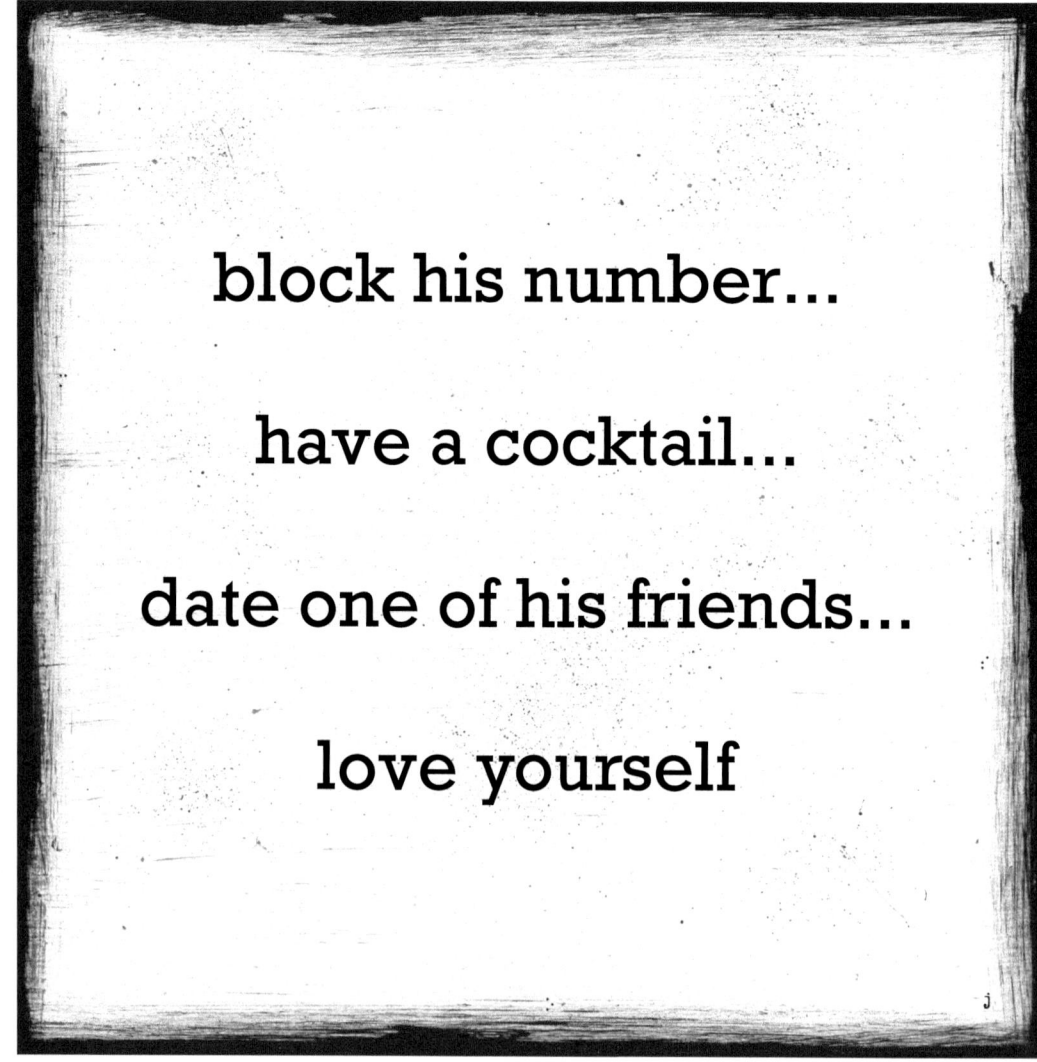

block his number...

have a cocktail...

date one of his friends...

love yourself

you are my person... and we are getting drinks

Guess what...
It just doesn't
make me
smile anymore...

and...
in the end...
karma will be
a bigger bitch
than me...

my inner child
is a mean little
shit...

then there's when
you accidentally
fuck someone for
three years...

my neighbor
just said "hi"
again...
I'm just going
to have to move.

and...
yes i can do
that...
but nah

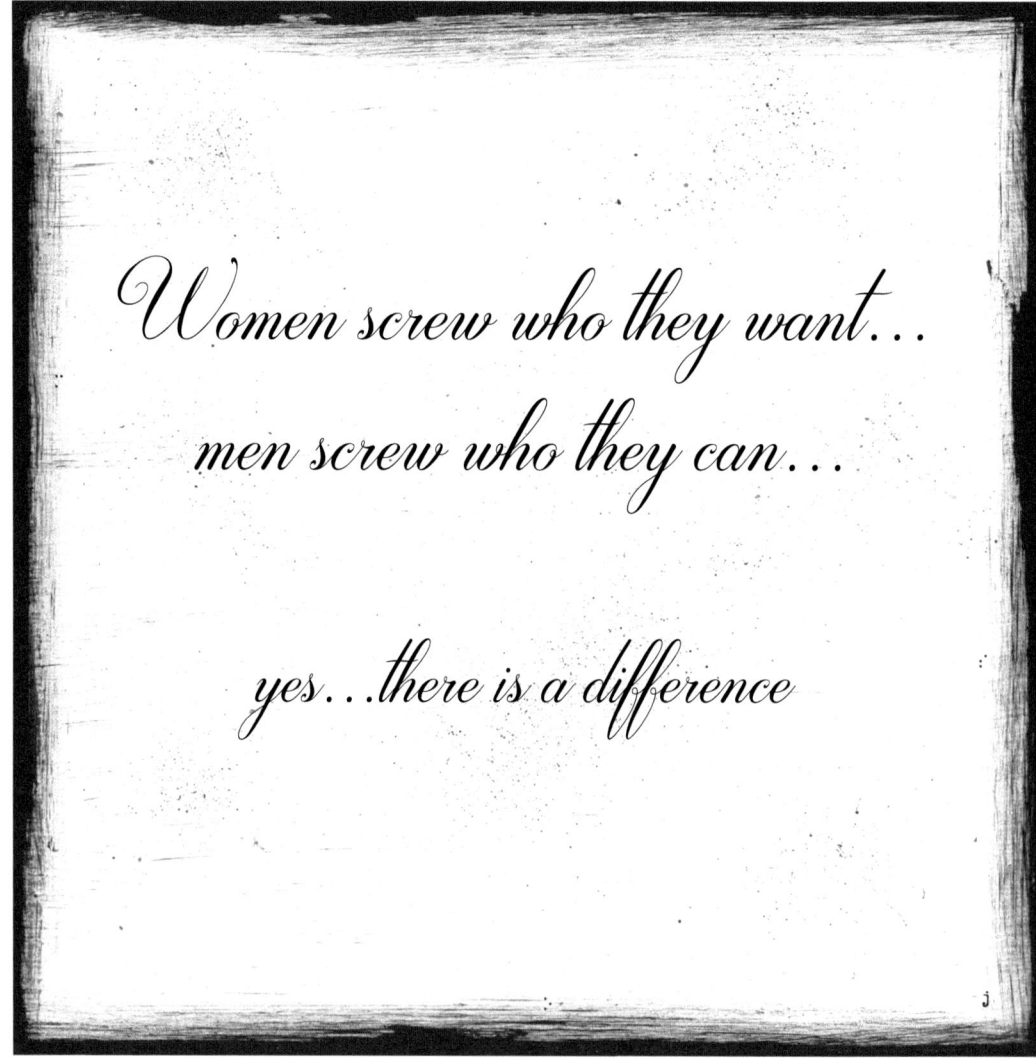

Women screw who they want…

men screw who they can…

yes…there is a difference

so fuck you/oh fuck/you're so
fucking late/hurry up fucker/
you are fucking kidding me/
pick a lane asshole/nice sig-
nal you fucking jerk/fuck off
i hate this fucking place/i
hate that fucking bitch/why
won't this fucking thing
work/oh fuck that hurt/if
that fucker calls me one more
time/answer the fucking ph/
i'm fucking broke again/i
don't want to fucking do this/

i hate that fucker/it's too fucking hot/it's fucking cold/it's fucking raining/look at that fucking snow/fuck no/fuck yes/there's no fucking pleasing them/let's get the fuck out of here/fuck this/ fuck that/help me do this fucking thing/fuck her/fuck him/where are my fucking glasses/just why the fuck not/what a fucking moron/fuck you and the horse you rode in on/he's a fucking jerk/now go out and tell someone to fuck off.

Actions
sometimes
show why
words mean
nothing

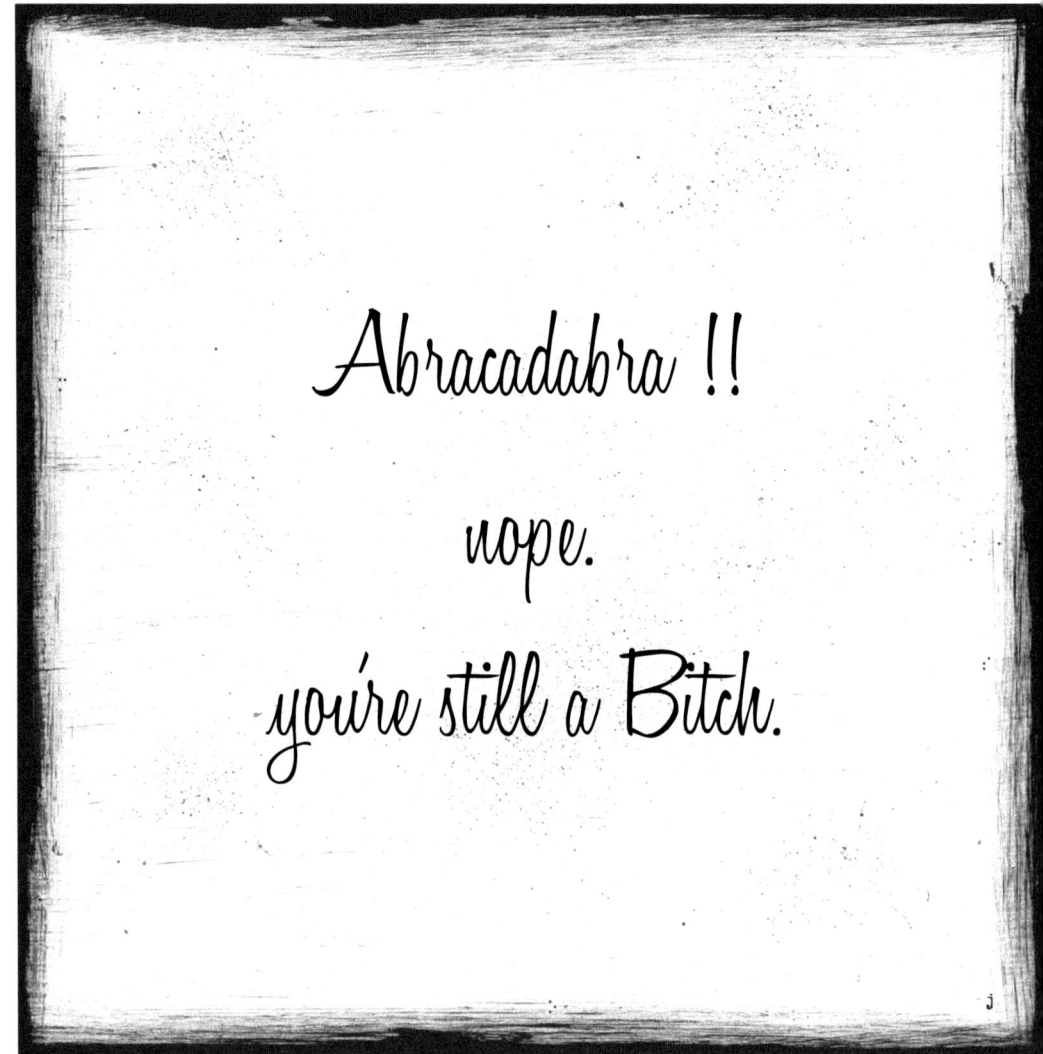

we don't care
about that
shit...
this time

if they don't text you
when they're drunk...
you ain't the one...

Just gave my last damn...

Nope...none left to give.

drunk in a room
with everyone
you've ever loved...
who do you go to
?

j

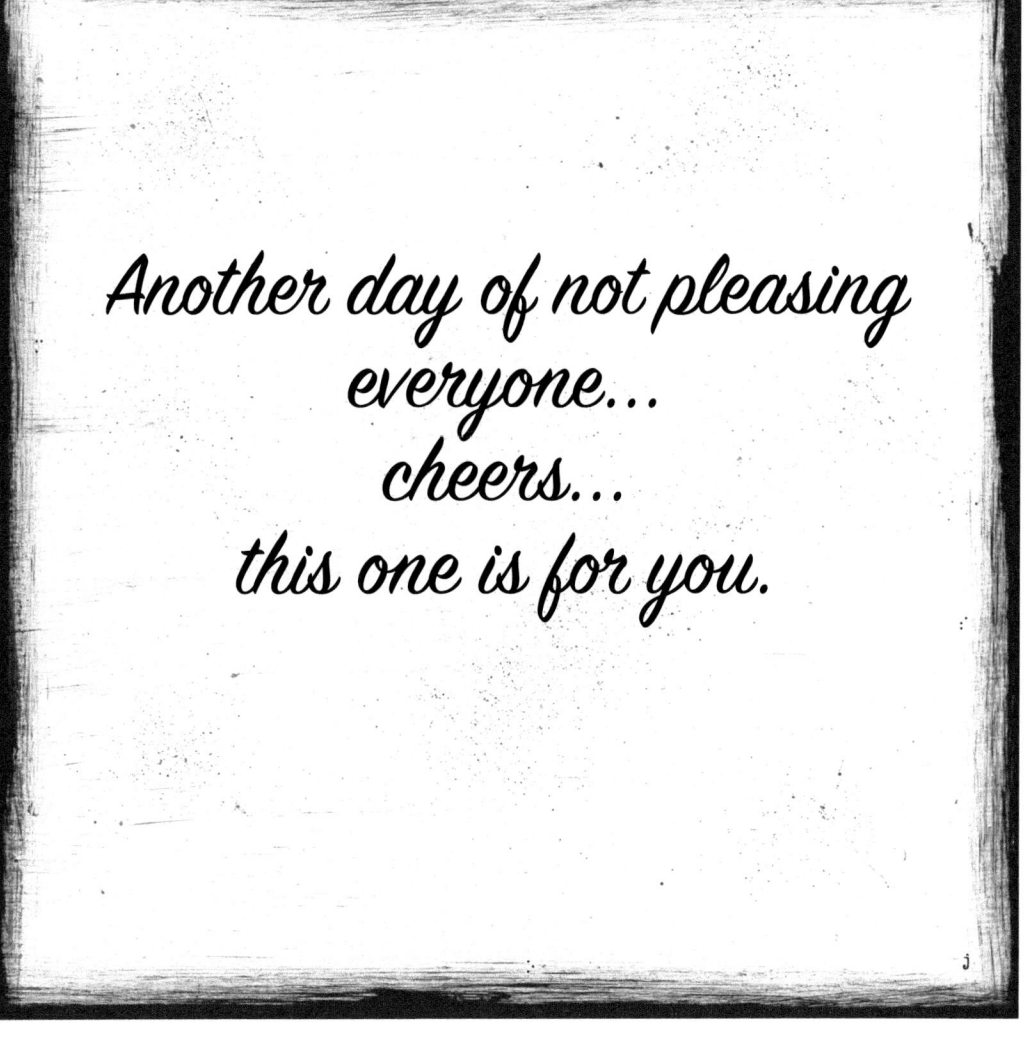

Another day of not pleasing everyone...
cheers...
this one is for you.

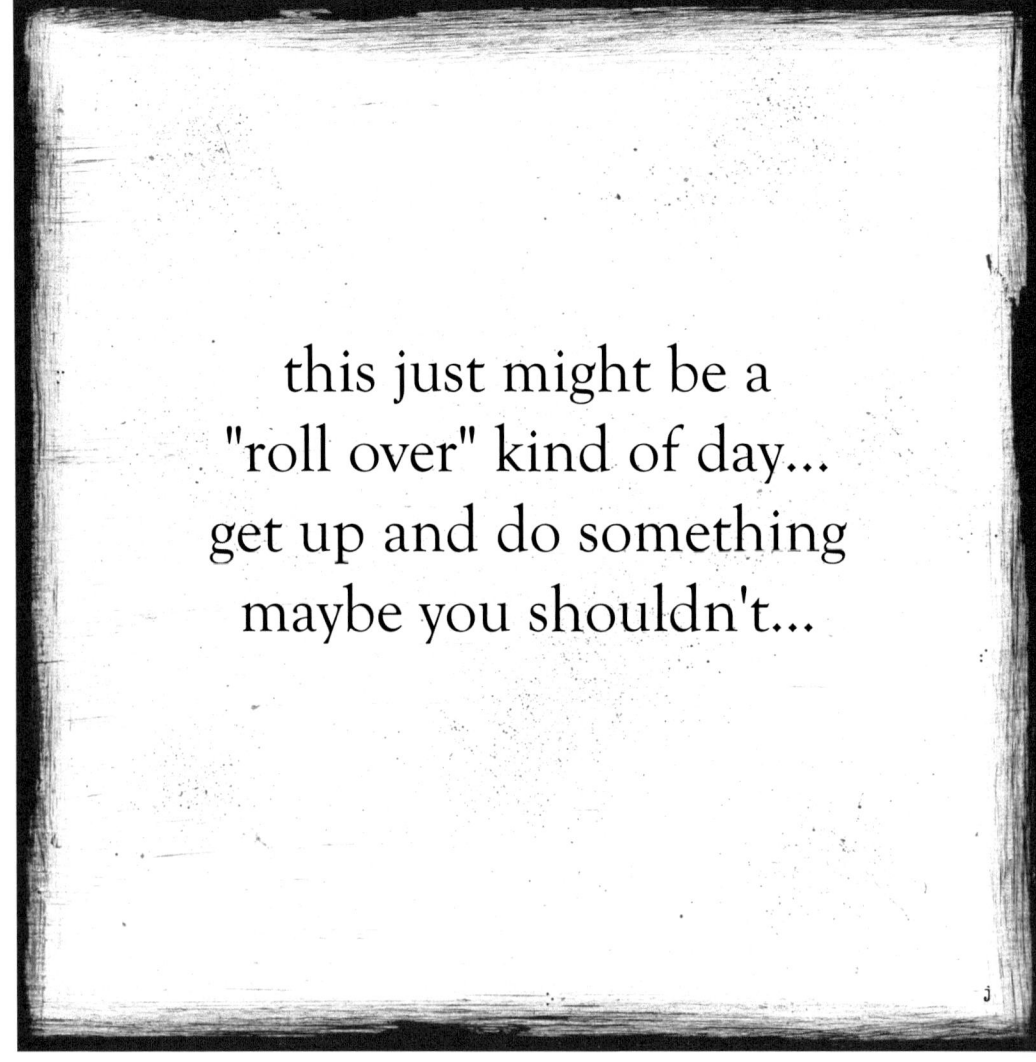

this just might be a
"roll over" kind of day...
get up and do something
maybe you shouldn't...

Heard you're a
player... nice
to meet you...
I'm the coach.

Silly Girl...
they
just
don't care...

328

aaaaaaaaaaaaaaaaaaaaaaaaaaaaaa
aaaaaaaaaaaaaaaaaaaaaaaaaaaaaa
aaaaaaaaaaaaaaaaaaaaaaaaaaaaaa
aaaaaaaaaaaaaaaaaaaaaaaaaaaaaa
aaaaaaaaaaaaaaaaaaaaaaaaaaaaaa
aaaaaaaaaaaaaaaaaaaaaaaaaaaaaa
aaaaaaaaaaaaaaaaaaaaaaaaaaaaaa
aaaaaaaaaaaaaaaaaahhhhhhhh...

fuuuuck.

a wise man
once said...
nothing

a wise woman
once said...
"fuck this shit"
and
she lived
happily
ever after.